Avon Almanac

Walking to School: Recollections of Bidford-on-Avon in the 1920s

Jack Moore

'There is history in all men's lives.'
(Henry IV, Pt2, Act 3, i, 80)

Editor: Roger Leese
Assistant Editors: Rodney Crompton, Bob Marshall
Sandra Parker and Mark Shaddick

Published by Bidford Publications 2023

Bidford and District History Society
Church House, Church Street, Bidford-on-Avon, Alcester, B50 4DA

Published by Bidford Publications
2023

ISBN 978-0-9575790-3-3

Designed by Chris Wheeler Graphic Design: www.chriswheeler.co.uk

Printed by CPI Antony Rowe: www. cpibooks.co.uk

Foreword

When telling the story of rural life in the twentieth century, historians are fortunate in having a wide range of printed sources from which to glean. They can also make good use of countryside images left by the increasing number of photographers, both amateur and professional, as the century wore on. But first-hand accounts of a period, a place or a series of events are far less common, and are rightly prized by those researching the recent past. First-hand testimony gives us the opportunity to gain an insight into everyday life – the mundane as much as the extraordinary. It can reveal the character, interests, thoughts and opinions of the writer. Through their writings we can join them in sharing humour and sadness, hardships and triumphs. They put the flesh on the bare, factual bones of history.

Jack Moore, whose writings form the centrepiece of this book, was certainly no ordinary schoolchild of the 1920s. His acute observation skills as a young lad in and around Bidford were every bit as accomplished as his ability to recall names, facts and incidents when committing his memories to paper nearly half a century later. In between these dates, he became an integral part of his village and was able to serve his community in a variety of ways, but his lasting legacy lies in these pages.

Through his words we are introduced to a cast of characters from the village, farms and hamlets. They move seamlessly around the neighbourhood and through the seasons - the children going to school, the farm workers to the fields, and shopkeepers to their High Street premises. The sights, sounds – and smells – of their activities are included in the narrative of a largely self-contained world that needed comparatively little from city or town.

Jack Moore, however, is quick to dispel any notion of life in the inter-war years being a rural idyll. He describes the hardships and privations endured by many, both young and old. There was no room for sentimentality in farming, either, with the economic pressures of the time. But throughout his writing his love and understanding of nature and its ways shines through.

This edition benefits from welcome additions from members of the Research Group of the Bidford and District History Society, who are to be commended on the thoroughness of their research. They introduce the author, set the period in context, guide us with local maps and illustrations and explain some of the more technical and dialect terms used in the Almanac, all to the reader's benefit.

We should be very grateful that Jack Moore had the foresight to record his memories of life between the wars. His was a story well worth telling, but all of us have something to share too. Future generations will be in our debt if at least some of us follow his lead and commit our stories to paper. In the meantime, do enjoy this journey back in time.

Robin Hill
Museums and Heritage Consultant
Malvern.

Preface

Jack Moore's *Avon Almanac* was originally self-published in 1972, three years before his death. The hand-written text was turned into typescript and hand bound in a laminated cardboard cover. Few additional copies appear to have been made. One was deposited with the Warwickshire County Record Office, the others presumably went to friends and family.

In this new edition, published by Bidford & District History Society, a short biography of Jack Moore, an introductory essay, extensive endnotes, and a glossary of technical and dialect terms have been added along with illustrations and a set of maps. This additional material is designed to place the *Almanac* in its wider historical context and to provide more detail on the people, places and aspects of village life referred to in the text.

Cherry Orchard, Bidford (*Permission of Rodney Crompton*)

Acknowledgements

This new edition of the *Almanac* is a product of ongoing research into the history of Bidford-on-Avon being undertaken by the Bidford & District History Society's Research Group under the Chairmanship of Wendy Shaddick, who has given enthusiastic support and encouragement to the *Almanac* project.

The Editorial team is especially grateful to Jack Moore's daughter, Elisabeth Green, for making available a copy of her father's original *Avon Almanac* and for providing valuable information about his life, especially his years as a market gardener in Bidford.

The team would also like to thank the following: Betty Hemming and Gabrielle Leese for their valuable research contributions; the late 'Pip' Handy for his assistance in explaining local dialect terms; Peter Chadwick of the Broom Research Group for granting access to the catalogued material on the Broom Jam factory in Irene Williams' Broom Scrapbook; John Alexander-Head for drawing attention to a press obituary of Jack Moore; and staff at Warwick County Record Office, Stratford-upon-Avon Archives and Library, and Evesham Library for making available relevant archive material.

Thanks are also due to Warwick County Record Office, the Shakespeare Birthplace Trust and Bomford Turner Ltd of Salford Priors for giving permission for photographic images in their possession to be included in the publication; to Max Taylor for his assistance with the front cover illustration; and to Gabrielle Leese for her careful proof-reading of the text.

The Research Group would also like to express its gratitude to the Bidford on Avon Parish Council for its generous financial support to this book which has enabled us to retain a retail price consistent with our last publication over four years ago.

The team is particularly grateful to Professor Malcolm Wanklyn and Professor John Benson for kindly reading drafts of the text and for offering constructive suggestions; Robin Hill for writing the Foreword; and, not least, Chris Wheeler, for designing the layout of the book.

List of Illustrations

The Bull's Head Inn (Permission of Rodney Crompton)
The Fisherman's Rest (Permission of Rodney Crompton)
The White Lion Hotel and Mason's Arms (Permission of Rodney Crompton)
Co-operative Society (Advert, Bidford Improvements Association, 1928)
Gray and Friend (Advert, Bidford Improvements Association, 1928)
Assembly Rooms (Permission of Rodney Crompton)
Noakes & Crofts (Advert, Bidford Improvements Association, 1928)
High Street, Bidford-on-Avon (Cowper's Series 6) (Permission of Rodney Crompton)
Holland's River Tea Garden and The River (Permission of Rodney Crompton)
Boats on the Avon (Permission of Rodney Crompton)
A Blenheim Orange (Wilhelm Lauche, Deutsche Pomologie. Wikimedia Commons)
Broom Junction (Permission of Rodney Crompton)
The Jam Factory, Broom, J.E. Williams 1977 (Permission of the Broom Research Group)
Bother'em Dick (ladies unknown) (Permission of Bob Marshall)
Broom Hall (Warwickshire County Record Office, PH21/62)
Money Meadow (Permission of Rodney Crompton)
Haymaking Marriage Meadows (Warwickshire County Record Office, PH21/61)
Tiger Tim's Weekly (Permission of Bob Marshall)
A typical wheelwright's workshop (Shutterstock: 1802710159)
Dr Crawford, with fellow surviving service men from Bidford after the First World War (We Will Remember Them. p162)
Stripped osiers drying by Bidford Bridge (Permission of Rodney Crompton)
Winnett's Butcher's High Spring Trap (Permission of Rodney Crompton)
Pleasure Boat Inn (Advert, Bidford Improvements Association, 1928)
Scratting Box (Permission of Avoncroft Museum)
An *old donkey driven press used in the cider making process* (Shutterstock 1438706771)
Broom Mill (Warwickshire County Record Office, PH21/59)
Billhook (Photograph: Mark Shaddick)
Bickmarsh Hall (Warwickshire County Record Office, EAC402)
Stanley Nailor (Advert, Bidford Improvements Association, 1928)
Planting Field Cabbages On A Smallholding (The Book of Market Gardening, R. Lewis Castle 1906 - Wikimedia Commons)

Every effort has been made to trace copyright ownership of the illustrations included. In some cases copyright has lapsed, in others investigations have proved inconclusive.

CONTENTS

Jack Moore and His Wife Mabel, 30th April 1939

(Permission of Elisabeth Green)

William John 'Jack' Moore

'Jack' Moore, as he was known locally, was born on 28th January, 1915, the eldest of five sons born to John Albert Moore and his wife Agnes (nee Osborne). The family lived in the old Manor House at 1 Icknield Street. His father was one of the Bidford 'Moore Brothers' who ran various small businesses in and around the village. John Albert established himself as a market gardener on land situated at the rear of the Manor House, the entrance to which lay between the Manor House and a small brick cottage (3 Icknield Street).

From an early age, Jack worked in the market garden with his father. On 30th April 1939 he married Mabel Houghton, the daughter of local stonemason, Fred Houghton, and set up home in the cottage at number 3. During the next six years they had three daughters, Mary, Elisabeth and Primrose. When Jack's mother, Agnes, became wheelchair bound, she and his father moved out of the Manor House into a new bungalow which his father built for them at the far end of Steppes Piece, in front of 'Moore Brothers Haulage Yard'. In his father's subsequent share out of his assets between his five boys, Jack, Edward Jesse, Raymond, Albert and Robert, Jack received the Manor House and the market garden. Such was the condition of the Manor House, however, that, according to Jack's daughter, Elisabeth, her mother refused to take her 'three little girls' into it, leading Jack to demolish the Manor House, and, with the help of German Prisoners of War, to build a new bungalow on the site.

Elisabeth recalls the market garden with affection:

> *The place was amazing, so many huge greenhouses and open land for root crops. I spent every hour I could with Dad. He was so generous. Anyone who came was given extra produce or a bunch of grapes from one of the two vines. He was also a very clever florist and I enjoyed helping him here too, spending many an hour beside him in the workshop wiring flowers for wreaths, bouquets and buttonholes. We had two*

specially heated greenhouses for exotic flowers and foliage for the floristry work, as well as for the arum lily he would grow for the Church at Easter time. Sadly, the Ministry of Agriculture came and destroyed these two greenhouses and forced us into growing more food for the war effort. In the photograph of their wedding you can see the bouquet my father made for his bride.

In the early fifties, she remembers, the market garden became 'a struggle' and 'we just kept it ticking over'. For several years, Jack tried to obtain planning permission for affordable houses to be built on the site, but this was only granted after his death, leading to the development of what became Icknield Close.

During the period of the market garden's decline, Jack took a job working on school playing fields in the South Warwickshire area and in his later years became Caretaker at Bidford High School. On one occasion, according to Bob Marshall, Jack caused a bit of a stir when, raking out the incinerator ashes, he found an unexploded World War 2 hand grenade. This resulted in a call to the Bomb Disposal Unit who came to remove it.

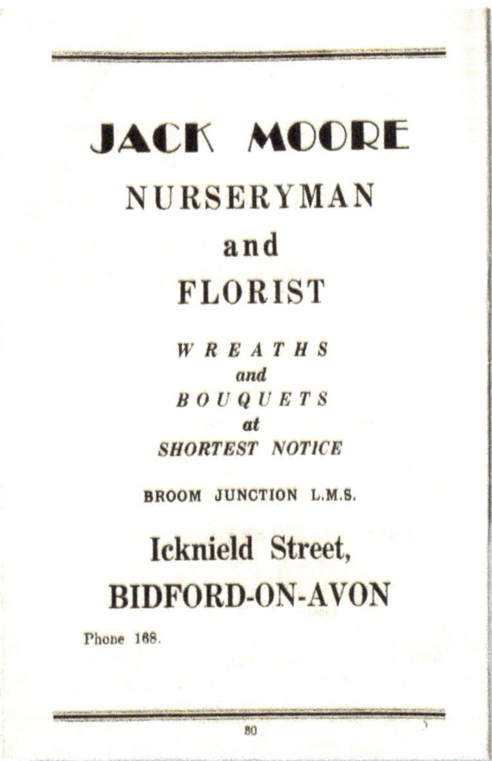

During World War II, Jack served in the National Fire Service, having joined as a volunteer in 1935. He continued as a retained fireman with Warwick County Fire Brigade when it became a County Brigade, before retiring in 1970 to become Sub-Officer in charge of Bidford Fire Station. Bob Marshall recalls one amusing incident involving Jack. He was just sitting down for his Sunday lunch when the house bells and the siren sounded for a call out. In those days the emergency fire call was made by tolling the bell at the top of Avon Cottage drive in Grange Road near to the Fire

JM Nurseryman and Florist
(Bidford Improvements Association, 1946)

Bidford Fire Service, 1960s. (Jack Moore pictured left)
(Permission of Bob Marshall)

Station. Jack arrived at the station, dressed in his fire kit and climbed into the seat reserved for the officer-in-charge. As the engine pulled out of the station, his wife Mabel stood waiting with his dinner. The plate was handed to him through the cab door and, with the fire bells ringing, Jack sat eating his roast dinner en route to a chimney fire in Salford Priors.

Jack had many interests outside work, none more important to him than his lifelong involvement with St Laurence Church. From an early age, he was a member of the choir and a keen bell ringer. His daughter, Elisabeth, joined him in the bell ringing when she was nine years old:

> *At New Year we would cover the clappers on the huge bell up in the top of the tower with muffles to give a solemn peal of bells to ring the old year out, then shortly before midnight we would scamper as fast as we could up the spiral stone stairs, take off the muffles and scoot back down through two floors into the ringing chamber at ground*

New Bells at St Laurence Church, 1960. Jack Moore pictured left in glasses
(Permission of Sandra Parker)

level to brightly ring in the New Year. Dad was always there, practice every week, every service, ceremonies of all sorts, weddings, and sad tolling of one bell for a sad occasion.

Her father also found and restored the hand bells and was instrumental in creating a young hand bell ringing group. He was a founder member of the Church of England's Men's Society as well as serving as a Churchwarden for 15 years. Being a keen woodworker, he was always turning his attention to something in the Church. His daughter remembers his talent for marquetry work, many pieces of which he gave to friends in the village.

Jack was one of the founders of the Bidford Improvement Society, and in 1935, to commemorate George V's Silver Jubilee, provided and, with the assistance of his brother Jesse, planted the avenue of chestnut trees from the entrance to the Big Meadow towards Marlcliff.

His interest in education extended well beyond his work on school playing fields. While working as Caretaker at the High School, he was Chairman of the Warwickshire Education Committee Consultative Council, and for 15 years was a Foundation Manager at Bidford Church of England Infant and Junior School.

Above all, Jack was a real countryman and lover of local history. The Almanac is Jack's own work which he wrote shortly before his death. It was typed for him by Joy Mayrick, who taught typing and shorthand at the High School. His death was sudden and unexpected. After working happily for several happy years as Caretaker at the School, Jack fell down the cellar steps one morning, as a result of which he suffered a brain injury and died a few days later in Warwick Hospital on 25th January, 1975, just three days before his 60th birthday. With him went a wealth of local knowledge which no doubt could have filled another book.

Avon Almanac

Introduction

Avon Almanac bears little resemblance to the yearly calendar of day to day events, anniversaries and astronomical data of the sort popularised by 'Old Moore'. This Moore's *Almanac* relates to the period of Jack Moore's schooldays which began in January 1920 when the four-year old Jack was admitted to Bidford Infants School in Church Street and ends when he left school at the age of 14 in 1929, having transferred to the Junior School in Victoria Road on 31 March 1922.[1] The *Almanac* comprises a collection of memories of those years, grouped around the seasons of the year and the journeys to school of boys from Bidford's outlying settlements, Cranhill and Broom to the north of the River Avon, and Barton, Marlcliff and Bickmarsh to the south.[2] The detail with which Moore invests these memories suggests that, although he himself lived in the centre of Bidford, he must have been familiar with these outlying lanes and pathways through his friendship with boys from these locations.

Moore's decision to commit his schoolboy memories to print may have been partly inspired by the publication of the first two books by the prolific Worcestershire writer, Fred Archer, who was born within three months of Moore. *The Distant Scene* (1967) and *Under the Parish Lantern* (1969) drew heavily on Archer's own early memories of life in and around Ashton-under-Hill, overlooking the Vale of Evesham. Even if Moore did not know Archer personally, it is likely that he would have been aware of these publications.[3]

In important respects, Jack Moore and Fred Archer exhibit similar characteristics in their writing. Both shared impressive powers of recall, a wide knowledge of the local landscape and a genuine feel for the rhythms of the countryside. In other ways, however, they were very different. The former's single publication contrasts markedly with Archer's prodigious output.[4] Whereas Jack remained a man of Bidford, well respected within his own community, Fred became a nationally known radio and television personality.[5] The two men also differed in their social and educational background. Jack came from artisan stock and received only an elementary education. Fred, on the other hand, grew up on his father's 500 acre farm and had the benefit of a grammar school education in Evesham. He developed a passion for literature and his books are sprinkled with numerous references to Shakespeare and to celebrated authors and poets such as Thomas Hardy and Matthew Arnold. He was also a great admirer of the 19th century Northamptonshire 'peasant poet', John Clare.[6] Such literary references are absent from the *Almanac.*

The two men's contrasting literary and educational backgrounds may also account for stylistic differences in their writing. One of the reasons for Archer's popularity is his attractively elegant style, whereas Moore's quirky sentence construction and punctuation at times detract from the *Almanac's* readability. This revised edition seeks to address these issues [7] and, by so doing, allow Moore's uniquely important insights into Bidford life in the 1920s to be more fully appreciated.

Pictured opposite:
Returning Bidford service men outside Lloyds Bank, 1919.
(Have You Forgotten Yet ? p.214)

The Almanac in Context

i. The Legacy of War

Jack Moore was born only one month after the prediction that the War would be 'all over by Christmas' had proved incorrect, yet no one then could have foreseen the horrific scale of the conflict to follow. The Bidford in which Jack grew up was markedly affected by the war. Recent research has shown that 69 out of the 357 Bidford men who fought in the conflict lost their lives and numerous survivors returned home with life-changing injuries.[8] Two members of the wider Moore family, Jesse and John Albert, however, appear to have returned from their period of active service relatively unscathed [9]. Nearly 47% of those who volunteered or were conscripted for the armed forces worked in agriculture or related trades, and the fact that most of the 15 appeals to Military Tribunals requesting exemption from conscription came from men employed on the land underlines the dependence of many families on agriculture for their livelihoods.[10]

Although much attention has focused on Lloyd George's promise to build 'homes fit for heroes' to live in, returning 'heroes' from rural communities regarded the provision of land as equally urgent. The government responded with the Land Settlement Act of 1919 which was primarily intended to create new farming opportunities for returning ex-servicemen. Across the country, County Councils bought up around 250,000 acres of land which were then divided into smallholdings for around 25,000 men, a mere 'drop in the ocean' compared with the 3.5 million demobbed between 1918 and 1922.[11] In Bidford, green corrugated huts were erected on various sites around the village, the Parish Council granted allotments to ex-servicemen on Friday Furlong, and ex-servicemen purchased many of the 54 plots created out of the 265 acres sold by Mrs Bradburn at Tower Hill Farm.[12]

An arguably more profound result of the economic and social dislocation brought about by the War was the government's decision to abandon its longstanding policy of free trade and introduce protection for agriculture. By late 1915, traditional sources of imported wheat such as the Black Sea region had dried up. In 1916, the North American harvest failed and extended U-boat activity in 1917 further exacerbated the problem.[13] As food prices rose, the government responded with the Corn Production Act of 1917. Farmers were instructed by County War Agricultural Committees[14] to plough up grassland and switch to cereal production. This and a guaranteed minimum price for wheat led to a rise of 1.86 million acres in the area under plough in England and Wales in the space of two years. The legislation also guaranteed a minimum wage for labourers, who, through the County Wage Boards, secured a voice for the first time in wage negotiations. Local farmers, although happy with the guaranteed prices, had reservations about the minimum wage:

> *Masters cannot afford to employ inefficient men and men incapable of doing a full day's work if they have to pay them the full standard wage.*[15]

Although the 1917 Act led to a temporary boom in agriculture at the end of the War, by the summer of 1920 foreign imports of wheat had resumed, leading to a fall in cereal prices and an unsustainable rise in government subsidies. This brief period of Government protection for agriculture ended in 1921 with an Act abolishing guaranteed prices for farmers and the guaranteed minimum wage for labourers. The Act passed into farming folklore as 'the great betrayal'.[16]

The withdrawal of government subsidies led to a general depression in agriculture which lasted for several years. Although all farming classes were affected, agricultural labourers probably suffered most.[17] Between 1921 and 1923, wages fell by nearly 40% compared with a fall in the cost of living of less than 30%. To make matters worse, by 1920 unemployment was rising as farmers began to lay off full-time employees and to stop using casual labour. Evidence of labourers on the move looking for work can be seen in the number of vagrants admitted to the Evesham Workhouse. This rose by 73 in one week alone in February 1920, by a further 69 in March and a further 50 in April.[18] Fred Archer recalled that during the early 1920s, 'everything slumped in price, especially corn'. Some farmers 'just let their land tumble down to grass' while others went in for market gardening, 'some growing a fair acreage of sprouts, others letting their fields to the more experienced Evesham growers'.[19] In his view, labourers were worse off than their fathers had been in the pre-War years.[20]

Good harvests in 1923 and 1924 and a levelling out of prices ushered in a period of modest recovery in the agricultural sector which lasted until the closing years of the decade. Moreover, the restoration by the Labour Government in 1924 of the County Wages Boards to set minimum wage rates helped to maintain a degree of stability in labourers' wages. There was no return, however, to the policy of protection, the government undertaking to assist farmers only as a means of alleviating rural unemployment.[21]

The war years witnessed a rapid growth in trade unionism within the labouring class, union membership rising from 10,000 in 1914 to 170,000 by 1919. However, the golden age of agricultural unionism in Warwickshire occurred during the Depression years of the 1870s. Originally formed in 1872 in Barford under the charismatic leadership of Joseph Arch,[22] the National Agricultural Workers Union had a membership of over 86,000 by 1874. However, a disastrous strike drained it of its funds and by 1889 membership had slumped to below 5,000. A more permanent local offshoot of the union movement at this time was the Bidford Co-operative Society. Formed in 1875, the Society celebrated its Golden Jubilee in 1925 by building the Co-operative Hall in the High Street which proved a welcome addition to the village's amenities.[23]

In the early 20th century the focal point of agricultural unionism shifted from Warwickshire to East Anglia.[24] Unionism in the Bidford and Evesham district in this period appears to have been less attractive and less confrontational than in the 1870s. Arguably, this was partly due to the growth of market gardening which was largely characterised by smaller units of production and relied more heavily on family labour.

Langston's home-grown asparagus (Barry Langston Collection, *Yesterday's Children*, p.63)

ii. The Growth of Market Gardening

For over 20 years before the outbreak of the War, Bidford had been experiencing changes in the balance of its farming economy which accelerated during the War and throughout Moore's childhood. The Great Depression from the 1870s to the mid-1890s resulted in widespread unemployment among the agricultural labouring class, fuelling a 'rural exodus' to the towns and industrial centres. Between 1872 and 1913 the area under crops in the UK fell from 24 million to less than 20 million acres, with the most serious decline in cereal-producing areas. By 1914 imported wheat accounted for over 70% of production.[25]

Bidford's population fell from 1575 in 1881 to 1369 by 1901, a drop of over 13%, suggesting a decline in employment opportunities and a consequent exodus to seek work elsewhere. No figures are available as to the number of labourers laid off. However, oral evidence from old Bidfordians at the turn of the century supports the view that many of

Bidford's adult male population struggled to find employment, especially those who worked on the land or in the building trade. [26]

Population decline was not uncommon among rural villages in the region at this time. Henry Rider Haggard, best known for his adventure stories such as *King's Solomon's Mines*, spent 1901 and 1902 travelling throughout rural England investigating the state of agriculture. He found that in Worcestershire many purely rural parishes had suffered population decreases since 1881.[27] The picture was more varied in south Warwickshire in the parishes adjacent to Bidford. The population in Salford Priors in 1901, for example, despite a fall in 1891, was slightly higher than it had been 20 years earlier, whereas the smaller parishes of Temple Grafton, Wixford and Exhall, suffered slight losses overall during the period. [28]

By contrast, in Evesham and nearby parishes such as Badsey a growth in employment opportunities saw their population rise significantly during the period[29] and helped to soften the impact of the Depression in the area. These increases derived from the expansion of market gardening and of fruit growing in particular from the 1850s onwards. By the turn of the century market gardening had overtaken farming as the predominant form of agriculture in the Vale.[30] This was not only due to improved techniques in manuring and planting which made the soil particularly suitable for the cultivation of fruit and vegetables,[31] but also to the effectiveness of developing sales organisations. Many producers were not large enough to sell direct to the market and opted to sell to larger growers or to collectives such as Littleton and Badsey Growers which was founded in 1908 and had members in the Bidford area.[32] Sale of the produce was also much aided by the construction of a rail network linking the region to markets in Cheltenham, South Wales, Birmingham and beyond.[33]

Bidford benefited from its proximity to the Vale of Evesham and the first four decades of the 20th century witnessed an increasing concentration of market gardening in the parish. By 1911 the earlier population losses had been reversed, the population having risen by 11.5% to 1636. Even in 1901 the Census had recorded as many as 50 market gardeners, representing 21% of the total workforce, comprising employees as well as employers and revealing the widespread use of family labour particularly on the smaller holdings. Trade Directories reflect the growing numerical dominance of market gardeners in the village over

Tower Hill Farm 1920
(Colin G Birt, Warwickshire Smallholders)

farmers.[34] The 1896 Directory listed eleven farmers and eight market gardeners. By 1912, however, the latter had overtaken the number of farmers and by 1936 were double their number. Crucial to these developments was the building of stations at Broom Junction (1879) and Bidford (1885) which became focal points for the transportation of local fruit and vegetables to more distant markets.[35]

The largest surviving farms in the Bidford area during the first 40 years of the 20th century were Tower Hill, farmed for most of the period by William Longford; Grange, which was worked successively by several different farmers; and Broom Court, the home of the Lane family until the late 1930s. In 1940 Grange and Broom Court Farms each exceeded 150 acres. However, the largest farmers in the area were the Blackwell family of Bickmarsh Hall.

By the 1920s, their 2,000 acres extended westwards to the Vale of Evesham and eastwards to the village of Dorsington.[36] A newspaper article in 1921 hailed the then owner, George Blackwell-Sims, as one of the 'prominent agriculturalists of Warwickshire', and not only praised his progressive farming methods and his innovative ideas for fostering better employer/employee relationships, but also noted the increasing acres dedicated to fruit and vegetables.[37] These acres amounted to market garden crops on a 'gigantic' scale compared with the characteristically much smaller holdings elsewhere in the region, and showed that, despite the large acreage still dedicated to 'livestock, cereals and hays', Blackwell Sims recognised the profits to be gained from market gardening and the potential safeguard it offered against further decline in the returns from cereal production.

The mid- and late-20s were characterised by a further expansion of fruit growing around Stratford-upon-Avon, Salford Priors and Bidford, and by improvements in methods of cultivation. With experiments showing conclusively that planting bush trees on cultivated land produced 'the highest possible percentage of first-grade fruits', demonstrations were held in 1925 on pruning, grafting and budding. These were 'attended by all classes' including farmers, smallholders, allotment holders, professional and amateur gardeners, teachers and scholars working in school gardens.[38]

Two years later, the distinguished writer on rural affairs, Samuel Bensusan,[39] visited Warwickshire. He confirmed the growing popularity of market gardening, observing 'a considerable increase in the area under raspberries and blackcurrants' around Salford Priors and Bidford', but also concluded that smallholders had to work 'very hard' in order to maintain a living, sometimes having to take on additional part-time work to make ends meet.[40]

Nevertheless, despite problems and setbacks, Growers Associations in the area continued to expand throughout the decade. In the early 1920s, two new Growers Societies were formed in the Bidford and Welford district,[41] out of which developed the much larger and influential Coventry Growers Sales Association. Reflecting on its growth in 1929, its Chairman, A H Hiller of Dunnington Heath Farm, admitted that, although the Association was now doing well, cooperative selling of fruit and vegetables was 'a very tough proposition' owing to the large number of people involved, and that, during the first three years of its existence it took the whole of its capital to keep it in business.[42]

In addition to economic uncertainty, the vagaries of the climate represented a further unpredictable factor affecting the livelihoods of those employed in fruit growing. The damage unseasonal weather could do to harvest prospects was reported in May 1927:

> *The prospect of a bumper fruit crop in Warwickshire has been considerably lessened by the frost of last Friday and Saturday. The loss will be a serious one for firms in the Bidford district...and will probably lead to a great deal of unemployment, as the damage done represents a big loss of capital to farmers, fruit farmers and market gardeners. Crops of all descriptions have been practically wiped out.*[43]

Themes in the Almanac:

Underlying the rich detail pervading the whole of the Almanac, three broad themes stand out:

i. Hardship

During Jack Moore's childhood, the expanding acreage dedicated to the cultivation of fruit and vegetables, allied to the rise in cooperative ventures, cushioned the Bidford district against the more violent fluctuations in the agricultural economy experienced in other areas. That 'Summer Hill Farm was in the depressed state of 'Dog and Stick' farming'[44] is his only overt reference to these wider trends. Nevertheless, the *Almanac*, directly or indirectly, regularly alludes to the hardships endured by many families and to the communal strategies employed to overcome them.

The reader is immediately confronted by the hardships associated with school attendance. Heating being confined to an open fire in each room, 'those unfortunates at the back of the class just shivered and any children who were sick with cold or plain hungry spent the day near the fire guard'.[45] These conditions were confirmed by the Junior School Headmaster, Mr Warner. In the School Log for 12 January, 1922, for example, he recorded the Main Room temperature at 9.00am as only 45 degrees, falling to 41 degrees the following day.[46] Attendance was very poor in wet weather. On a particularly wet morning on 20 December 1922, Warner was 'obliged to dry clothes for many children and send home three who were soaked to the skin'.[47]

Such conditions undoubtedly contributed to the widespread occurrence of infectious and contagious diseases, especially during the winter months. When numbers reached epidemic proportions, as with the outbreak of influenza in November 1918,[48] and diphtheria in November 1924,[49] the school was closed. In November 1925, two cases of scarlet fever were diagnosed in addition to 'many bad coughs and colds'.[50] Children were also excluded for contagious skin infections and hair infestations such as impetigo and nits. In October 1926, the visiting nurse, Miss Hodges, found several pupils in the lower classes to be 'very dirty' and others whose hair was in poor condition.[51]

In winter, children from the outlying settlements brought with them a basic diet of bread and jam and a bottle of cold tea or cocoa. In the summer months they usually had water to drink, obtained from a pump in the Headmaster's yard. This, Moore recalls, 'was the extent of school meals and refreshment' except for the last day of the Christmas term when each pupil was given a bar of chocolate.[52] On one of the rare occasions in the Almanac when he compares conditions in his childhood with those at the time of writing, he sums up the hardships many Bidford children of his generation experienced:

> *the red-faced and healthy-looking school child of today is vastly different from some of the wizened faced hungry children in handed-down clothes ... when a cure for whooping cough was to stand near the tar boiler and inhale the noxious fumes.*[53]

Moore is largely silent on conditions within the home except to refer to the garden-end privies and the outdoor pump supplying the water, which was likely to freeze up in winter. Furthermore:

> *When filling a kettle [from a pump] in the dark, it was a good idea to give the handle a few jerks. Turgid black slugs used the spout for overnight somnolence and to fill the kettle with the first water, one ran the risk of the taste of boiled slug in the early cup of tea.*[54]

One of the ways for a family to supplement its income, especially during times of unemployment or reduced hours of work, was by renting an acre or so in the communal allotments in order 'to grow a piece of wheat, a pole or two of potatoes and a couple of rows of plums'.[55] A further means of mitigating hardship was by participation in pea picking, 'an important labour necessary to shoe and clothe the family before winter set in',[56] the money earned often being used to purchase homespun cloth for turning into winter clothes such as balaclava helmets and hand-knitted mittens.[57] Schools in many rural areas allowed designated periods for children to assist in this activity, accepting the reality that if they tried to enforce attendance, families would keep their children away from school

Pea Pickers in Broom.
(Warwickshire County Record Office - PH350/250)

anyway. Holidays were fixed to coincide with the pea picking season. In 1918, Bidford Infant School closed for the 'Pea Picking Holidays' on 19 June and reopened on 15 July, although the School Log noted on 14 June that some children had already been staying away.[58] Moore recalls that several mothers would bring prams with false bottoms, 'allowing the base to be filled with a few boilings of peas and the baby put back to sleep over them'.[59]

Another important activity to supplement families' food supply was the ritual of the pre-Christmas pig killing. This was very much a shared benefit within the community, since 'the helpers had a share of the cut meat and, when their killing came, theirs would be shared out also'.[60]

ii. The Old and the New

Mechanisation advanced rapidly during the Victorian period in the large arable regions of southern and eastern England, where by the end of the 19th century virtually all harvesting was being undertaken by machines.[61] However, in market gardening areas like the Vale of Evesham and Bidford, fields were generally too small and irregular for largescale mechanisation, although some smallholders might manage to hire machinery for a few days at a time, usually as part of a collective arrangement with other smallholders.

The *Almanac* brings out clearly the ways in which established methods of farming continued to flourish in the Bidford area during the 1920s alongside the growth of mechanisation. This can be seen especially in the continuing importance of horses in the village economy. Martin Pugh points out that 'despite the use of 25,000 tractors, steam engines for ploughing, self-binders and reaper-binders on farms, the role of the horse was only gradually being eroded', and calculates that as many as 668,000 horses, mainly shires, were still working on British farms in 1939.[62] Moore details numerous activities in which horses played an essential role, including haymaking,[63] harvesting,[64] drawing timber wagons,[65] and carting slag from Bidford Siding for road maintenance.[66]

As for non-agricultural village traders, carriers like Tom Taylor and Elijah Bryan still used a horse and dray, as did Davis's, the monumental masons.[67] The trap belonging to Winnetts's Butchers was horse-drawn and Charles Dowdeswell's saddler's shop in the High Street, which remained in business until the late 1930s, underlined the continuing importance of the horse in village life.[68]

Mechanisation was more in evidence on the larger farms. By 1921 two steam ploughs were responsible for most of the ploughing on the Bickmarsh estate,[69] although Moore remembers 'many horses and wagons' working there.[70] Longford's farm on Tower Hill owned a steam plough and a 'great Tangye Gas Engine' which was used for 'driving farm

J. Cousien Sculff Engraving of John Linnell's Painting of Agricultural Labour (1865)
(Wellcome Library no. 30091i)

machinery, chaff-cutting, root chopping and log sawing'.[71] Fred Archer's 500 acre farm at Ashton-under-Hill invested in a mowing machine and a mechanical reaper and seed-drill, but horses continued to be integral to the farming process. The mowing machine and seed-drill were both horse-drawn and the four-horse plough remained a common sight throughout the decade.[72]

Motorised transport was increasing. Charabancs had been bringing visitors to Bidford since the first decade of the century.[73] Following the collapse of his Canning Company, George Crompton, ever alert to new entrepreneurial opportunities, set up his Reliance Bus Company in 1927, which together with its rival, the Stratford Blue Buses, provided Bidford residents with convenient access to nearby Evesham and Stratford-upon-Avon.[74] Private cars, however, remained a relative novelty. Among those attracting special attention were Dr Crawford's big yellow Sunbeam and Gilbert Boshier's red open top Talbot.[75] Like Crompton, Boshier epitomised those entrepreneurs who recognised the potential of motorised transport. First appearing in the Trade Directories in 1916 as a cycle agent, by 1921 he had opened a motor garage and, according to Moore, also operated a 'fashionable taxi service'.[76] Similarly alert to new opportunities, Ernest Wilkes swapped his butcher's business for that of motor car hirer.[77] Cars were not the only form of motorised transport to catch the eye. The newsagent, William Jones, 'could be seen

An advert for the Reliance Bus Company in the Bidford Improvements Association Horse Races and Sports Carnival Official Programme, Thursday 9th August 1928.
(Bidford Improvements Association, 1928)

careering out of his back entrance on his round tank BSA and sidecar to meet the 7.55am train to Broom to collect the village papers and periodicals'. [78]

From an early age Jack was fascinated by how things operated, and one of the *Almanac's* most valuable legacies to the historian is the immense detail devoted to his descriptions of machines and farming methods. Fred Archer's prolific output is littered with detailed recollections of life on the land, but even he cannot match Jack Moore when it comes to depicting the innermost workings of mechanised equipment. Nowhere is this better illustrated than in Moore's account of the intricate operation of 'steam scuffling', a process better known today as 'scarifying'.[79]

This degree of detail is similarly evident in his descriptions of traditional practices such as threshing,[80] haymaking,[81] osier rod peeling,[82] shoeing horses,[83] and hedging and ditching.[84] Furthermore, his intimate knowledge of the processes involved in harvesting suggests his personal participation in tasks to which boys were often assigned, such as bond tying, bundling the sheaves and assisting with the scuffling.[85]

The Almanac's most graphic description, however, is of the annual pre-Christmas pig-killing ritual.[86] Not for the faint-hearted, the account details every stage in the process, from the family's preparation to the killing of the pig and the systematic dissection of the dead animal, ensuring that no part of it went to waste. Rearing a pig for killing before Christmas was an age-old tradition stretching right across Europe.[87] Writing of her 1880s childhood on the Oxfordshire-Northamptonshire border, Flora Thompson stresses the importance of the pig to the domestic economy. During its lifetime the pig was 'an important member of the family', but, in a description of the pig killing no less graphic than Moore's, admitted that 'country people of that day had little sympathy for the suffering of animals', especially when what they provided was such a crucial element in a family's yearly food supply.[88]

iii. The Natural World

For all Jack Moore's impressively detailed knowledge of machines and the seasonal round of agricultural tasks, what stands out above all in the *Almanac* is his close affinity with the natural world. From exploring with his boyhood friends, Moore came to know the local countryside intimately and his encounters with the natural world inspired some of his most evocative and eloquent passages. The railway track near Summer Hill Farm was the site of particularly vivid memories:

> *The banks of the track were a haven for grass snakes and glinting kingfishers and goldfinch feeding in groups on the numerous thistle heads...* [89]

On a summer night around Grafton Lane:

> *the sun-warmed sleepers of the railway track would glisten with masses of glow-worms, so much so that the fire brigade was called out because someone passed by and thought the sleepers were embering with ghostly fire.* [90]

He was well-versed in local folklore, especially that relating to weather forecasting:

> *A fine day was certain if the Ragley rooks were flying high away to the Cotswolds instead of hanging around locally if tempest or rain was expected...*[91]

Spiders strengthening their webs in the hedgerows were a sure indication of squally weather

to come,[92] and a hard winter was likely when 'the hedges were festooned with old man's beard and gaudy with hips and haws'.[93] Mention of Caroline Osborne's bees prompts a recitation of the mantra that 'the swarms of May' were worth 'a load of hay', 'the swarms of June... a silver spoon', the 'swarms of July...not worth a butterfly'.[94]

The *Almanac* is alive with sound and movement, whether in the descriptions of people engaged in their work, the sounds of machines, such as the 'tump, tump' of the Tangye Gas Engine,[95] or the sounds of the natural world, heard, for example, in 'the scurry of water vole, sly and silent otter or a clackety dispersal of moorhens or dabchicks across the river to the safety of the majestic elms'.[96]

Moore's most seamless fusion of sights and sounds, however, occurs in his description of night-time activities in 'Winter Cranhill'.[97] This, more than any other passage, reflects a man deeply attuned to the rhythms of the countryside with his own distinctive flair for bringing it to life:

> *It was the time for nightly prowling with bat fowling nets, watching where an odd pheasant went to roost, checking over the long rabbit nets and bolting the holes with slipped in ferrets, with the resultant merciless squeal as they reached the bottom burrows. Time also on a quiet night for the bloodcurdling howl of the vixen and the banshee flight of the great ghostly barn owl.*

Almanac Introduction

Endnotes

1. The School Register does not record his precise date of departure.
2. Although it features prominently in the Almanac, Bickmarsh was not part of Bidford parish. In 1894 it became a parish in its own right, comprising what had formerly been the Warwickshire portion of the parish of Welford-on-Avon.
3. Archer was encouraged to publish his memories by the Gloucestershire author, John Moore (1907-1967), who is widely regarded as the leading writer on rural life of his generation. He is best known for his trilogy, set in and around Bredon Hill: *Portrait of Elmbury*, based on his home town of Tewkesbury; *Brensham Village; and The Blue Field.*
4. 22 more books followed during the next three decades, the only one of these to adopt an almanac format being *A Country Twelvemonth* (1992).
5. His appearances became increasingly gimmicky, not least his talking to Samantha Fox in a horse trough and singing with a pig in Selfridges to promote his latest book.
6. F Archer: *Hay Days* (2001), Introduction, p. ix. Auberon Waugh's claim that Archer was 'the authentic voice of the English peasantry' seems misplaced given the fact that Archer was born into the farming class. More deserving of the credit was the Northamptonshire 'mad poet', John Clare (1793-1870), so-called because he spent the last 33 years of his life in a mental asylum. Like his father, Clare never rose beyond the rank of agricultural labourer, but his poetry far transcended his lowly working status and he was described by his biographer, Jonathan Bate, as 'the greatest labouring-class poet that England has ever produced' (Jonathan Bate: *John Clare: a Biography*, (2003)
7. See Notes on the Revised Text for a discussion of editing criteria.
8. B Marshall, *We Will Remember Them* (2014); B Marshall, *Have You Forgotten Yet?* (2018).
9. *Have You Forgotten Yet?*, pp. 144-145.

10. *We Will Remember Them*, pp. 166-167; *Have You Forgotten Yet*, pp. 231-234, 240-241.
11. R Munday, 'How Farming Suffered post-WW1 from Government's 'Great Betrayal', in *Farmer's Weekly*, November 2018, www.fwi.co.uk/news/how-farming-suffered-post-WWI-from-governments-betrayal
12. *Have You Forgotten Yet?*, p. 219.
13. A Howkins, *Reshaping Rural England: A Social History, 1850-1925 (1991)*, pp. 254-255.
14. They were originally set up in 1915 as the County Agricultural Committees but lacked executive power until the Act of 1917. The 'War Ags', as they came to be known, were re-established in 1939.
15. *Evesham Journal*, 24 April, 1920.
16. Munday, *op cit.*
17. Howkins, *op cit.*, p. 283.
18. *Evesham Journal*, 24 April, 1920.
19. F Archer, *Under the Parish Lantern*, (1969), p. 56.
20. F Archer, *Grain and Chaff under the Hill*, (1991), p. viii.
21. H Newby, *Country Life: A Social History of Rural England* (1987), pp. 169-170.
22. Arch visited Bidford on at least five occasions between 1872 and 1884. A branch of the Union was formed in 1872 with about 50 members after a visit by the Union's Secretary, W Stratford. Arch's first visit appears to have taken place shortly afterwards, as a result of which membership rose to 320. In March 1877, the Union held a dinner and business meeting in 'a very spacious tent' in the grounds of the Pleasure Boat Inn before Arch headed a procession through the streets which attracted a crowd of about 1,000. Arch addressed further meetings at the Pleasure Boat in 1880, 1883 and 1884, by which time the Union was experiencing a decline in support. Arch himself, however, was still capable of attracting large crowds. His visit in 1884 saw him campaigning for the extension of the vote to the rural labouring class and drew around 1,000 labourers to the yard of the Pleasure Boat (*Alcester Chronicle*, 17 March, 1877; 26 June, 1880; 4 August, 1883. *Birmingham Daily Post*, 2 May, 1884).
23. *Evesham Journal*, 8 August 1925.
24. Howkins, *op cit.*, p.268.
25. L Margaret Barrett, 'English Food Policy during the First World War' (1985), p.3; Jonathan Brown, 'Agriculture in England. A Survey of Farming' (1987), p.10, in

A. Howkins, *Reshaping Rural History: A Social History*, 1850-1925 (1991), p.252.

26. R Churchley, 'Hard Times in Bidford-on-Avon', *Local Past*, Winter 1981/2, Alcester Historical Society.
27. Henry Rider Haggard (1856-1925) spent the years between 1875 and 1882 in South Africa as a government official, becoming Registrar of the High Court in the Transvaal in 1878, the year following its annexation by the British. When he returned to England in 1882, his time was increasingly taken up with the writing of adventure stories. For his Allan Quatermain novels he drew his inspiration from the colourful characters he had encountered in Africa. *King Solomon's Mines*, published in 1885, was soon followed by *Allan Quatermain* and *She*, one of the best-selling novels of all time. Another of his interests was agricultural reform and he was member of numerous royal commissions on land use. During his travels around rural England, he stayed for a few days in June 1901 with John Idiens of Wickhamford Manor in Worcestershire and spoke to several leading agriculturalists in the area. See extract from *Rural England* in The Badsey Society (https://www.badseysocietyuk/market-gardening-and-farming/rider-haggards-agricultural-survey-the-vale-evesham)
28. In 1881, the population of Salford Priors stood at 823, falling to 780 in 1891 before rising to 828 ten years later.
29. Evesham's population rose from 5,112 in 1881 to 7,101 in 1901, that of Badsey from 442 to 775 during the same period. Employment opportunities for out of work rural labourers continued to be offered by the large industrial towns to the north. Birmingham's population increased from 400,774 in 1881 to 522,204 in 1901, that of Coventry from 56,813 to 88,107. However, some other towns which lacked an industrial base or, unlike Evesham, were not situated at the centre of an expanding agricultural region, suffered a loss in population. Stratford-upon-Avon's population, for example, fell from 58,954 to 55,130 during the period and continued to decline until 1931.
30. Howkins, op cit., p. 213.
31. Bidford and District History Society, *Yesterday's Children* (1913), p. 56.
32. C A Binyon, *The LBG Story* (1958). One such local member was Hillers of Dunnington Heath Farm.
33. *Yesterday's Children*, p. 57.
34. Unlike the Censuses, Trade Directories do not provide a comprehensive occupational record, since they normally only included employers, the self-employed and those

living by independent means. Moreover, since Directories like Kelly's charged a small fee for entry, a number of small traders especially chose not to be listed. Nevertheless, broad trends such as the farmer/market gardener ratio are discernible.

35. The Day Book of a Bidford market gardener, thought to be Jesse Houghton (1851-1921), reveals that as early as 1900 his plums were not only finding regular markets in Evesham and Stratford but were also being sold in Birmingham and Manchester. Between 1915 and 1920 markets had expanded to include Leeds, Liverpool, Hull and Glasgow, the produce having been 'put on rail' at Broom Junction (Warwickshire County Record Office, CR2191/3).
36. A further 400 acres were farmed at Saintbury.
37. *Leamington Spa Courier*, 10 June, 1921.
38. *Tamworth Herald*, 25 July, 1925. There is nothing recorded in Bidford Junior School Log to indicate that teachers and pupils participated in this training, although, according to the *Almanac* (p. 43), the boys did work in the school gardens.
39. Samuel Levi Bensusan (1872-1958) was born in Dulwich, the son of a Jewish feather merchant. Samuel took a keen interest in country matters and bought a farm in Essex, H G Wells, Thomas Hardy and the composer, Gustav Holst being among his near neighbours. A prolific writer, he wrote at least 25 books on agricultural topics and was regularly employed by various newspapers across the country to review the state of agriculture in their locality. His travels took him over 4,000 miles and provided him with a wealth of material for his most well-known publication, *Latter Day Rural England* (1927).
40. *Warwick and Warwickshire Advertiser*, 13 August, 1927.
41. *Ibid*, 5 February, 1921. The names of these Associations are not recorded, although Hillers at Dunnington Court Farm was almost certainly involved.
42. *Ibid*, 2 February, 1929.
43. *Ibid*, 7 May, 1927.
44. *Almanac*, p. 71. See also Glossary, 'Dog and Stick' farming'.
45. *Ibid*, p. 43.
46. CR1153/2 Bidford Junior School Log Book, 1913-1923, 12 January, 1922.
47. Ibid, 20 December, 1922.
48. CR2376/1 Infant School Log Book, 1918-1932, 18 November, 1918.
49. 'Annual Report of the Medical Officer of Health, Alcester', *Evesham Standard* and *West Midland Observer*, 27 June 1925

50. Infant School Log Book, op cit, 12 November, 1925.
51. Junior School Log Book, op cit., 6 October, 1926.
52. *Almanac*, p. 43.
53. *Ibid*, p. 100.
54. *Ibid*, p. 43.
55. *Ibid*, p. 45.
56. *Ibid*, p. 53.
57. *Ibid*, pp. 99-100.
58. Infant School Log, op cit., 14 June and 19 June, 1918.
59. *Almanac*, p. 80. Oral testimony recalling the early years of the century refers to the contribution made by women to the family economy from their income as domestic outworkers for needle and glove manufacturers in Alcester. The fact that such outworking was in decline by the 1920s may possibly explain why it does not find mention in the *Almanac* (Churchley, 'Hard Times in Bidford-on-Avon' op cit).
60. *Ibid*, p. 104.
61. Newby, *op cit.*, pp. 72-74.
62. M Pugh, *Shall We Dance? A Social History of Britain between the Wars* (2009), p. 261.
63. *Almanac*, p.p. 71-74.
64. *Ibid* pp. 88-90.
65. *Ibid* p. 49.
66. *Ibid*, p. 50.
67. *Ibid*, pp. 75-76.
68. *Ibid*, p. 53.
69. *Leamington Spa Courier*, 10 June 1921.
70. *Almanac*, p. 63.
71. *Ibid*, p. 48.
72. F Archer, *A Country Twelvemonth*, pp. 38, 50, 53, 85.
73. *Yesterday's Children*, p. 88.
74. *Ibid*, pp. 67-68.
75. *Almanac*, p. 49.
76. *Ibid*, p. 57.
77. *Kelly's Directory, Warwickshire*, 1921 and 1924
78. *Almanac*, p. 54. PC Munday also sported a motor cycle combination with sidecar (p.52.)

79. *Ibid*, pp. 90-91.
80. *Ibid*, pp. 51-52.
81. *Ibid*, pp. pp. 72-74.
82. *Ibid*, pp. 59-60, 81.
83. *Ibid*, p. 78.
84. *Ibid*, p. 100.
85. *Ibid*, pp. 88-91.
86. *Ibid*, pp. 102-104. Shorter in length, but equally bloody in content, are the descriptions of a pig-killing in the slaughter house of the butcher, George Winnett (p. 58), and the killing and plucking of poultry in the lead-up to Christmas (p. 104).
87. F Archer, *Under the Parish Lantern*, p. 100.
88. F Thompson, *Lark Rise to Candleford*, (1979 edition), pp.10-12.
89. *Almanac*, p. 71.
90. *Ibid*, p. 74.
91. *Ibid*, p. 44.
92. *Ibid*, p. 83.
93. *Ibid*, p. 99.
94. *Ibid*, p. 85.
95. *Ibid*, p. 48.
96. *Ibid*, p. 81.
97. *Ibid* p. 99. 'The rabbit has always been the countryman's quarry'. Before 1880, tenants were prohibited from killing rabbits on their own land. However, following a successful lobbying campaign highlighting the extensive damage which rabbits did to crops, an Act of Parliament legalised the practice. Ferreting was found to be a more effective method than traps in reducing numbers. (F Archer, *Under the Parish Lantern*, p. 114).

Notes On The New Edition

The guiding principle underpinning this new edition of *Avon Almanac* is to enhance its readability whilst preserving the authentic voice of Jack Moore. With this in mind, various amendments have been made to Moore's text where these were deemed necessary or desirable. One of the characteristics of Moore's style of writing, especially when describing mechanical or agricultural processes, is his tendency to use extremely long sentences where the grammatical structure breaks down and a clear sense of the meaning is lost. In this edition such passages have been altered to achieve greater coherence. This has often been possible by simply deleting 'and' or 'but', and by a more strategic insertion of commas. In a few instances, however, some limited rewriting has been necessary in the interests of grammatical correctness. The opening sentences of the Almanac as they were originally written are one instance where some reconstruction has taken place.

Spelling inconsistencies have been ironed out, for example, 'osiernate' being preferred to 'osienate'. These, however, number very few as do errors in transcription. 'On' is occasionally typed instead of 'in', but, overall, Moore's typist, Joy Mayrick, is to be congratulated on so accurately transcribing his hand-written text.

Where it is concluded that Moore uses a word which gives a different meaning from that which he intended to convey, an alternative word has been substituted. For example, his use of the phrase, 'choice Brummies', has been changed to 'choosy Brummies'. Importantly, there are some words which on first reading might appear to qualify for this category, but which prove to be dialect terms, some dating back nearly 200 years. One such example is 'mauling', a dialect word which means 'to move along wearily or with difficulty', and used by John Clare in *The Shepherd's Calendar*, originally published in 1827.

In summary, a very large proportion of the original text of the *Almanac* has been preserved unaltered in the new edition, and what amendments have been made have not undermined the distinctive style and character of this rich historical source which illuminates so vividly a hitherto neglected period in Bidford's history.

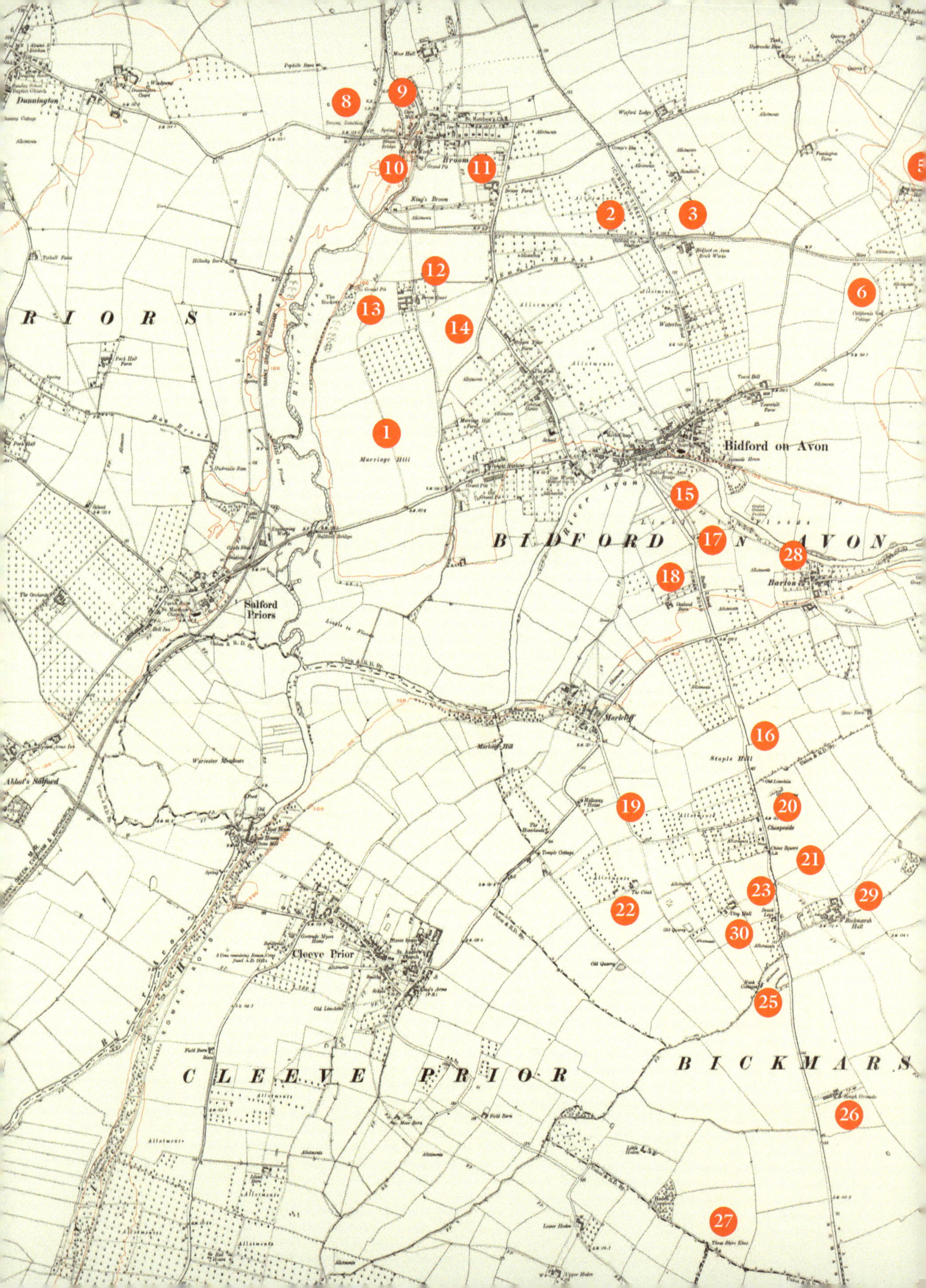
Dunnington
Broom
King's Broom
R I O R S
Marriage Hill
Bidford on Avon
B I D F O R D
A V O N
Barton
Salford Priors
Abbot's Salford
Worcester Meadows
Marlcliff
Marlcliff Hill
Staple Hill
Cleeve Prior
C L E E V E P R I O R
B I C K M A R S
Bickmarsh Hall
1
2
3
5
6
8
9
10
11
12
13
14
15
16
17
18
19
20
21
22
23
25
26
27
28
29
30

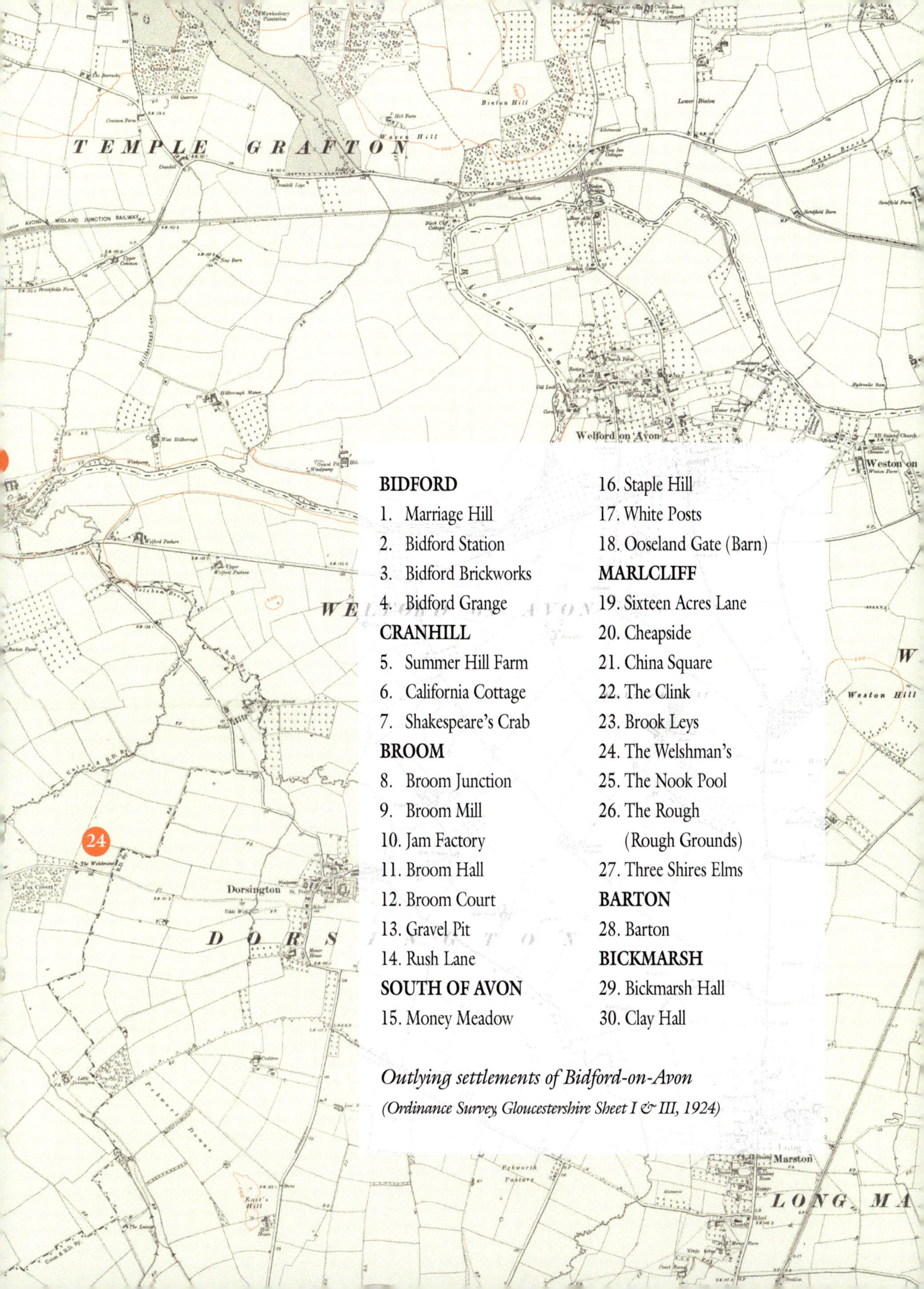

BIDFORD
1. Marriage Hill
2. Bidford Station
3. Bidford Brickworks
4. Bidford Grange

CRANHILL
5. Summer Hill Farm
6. California Cottage
7. Shakespeare's Crab

BROOM
8. Broom Junction
9. Broom Mill
10. Jam Factory
11. Broom Hall
12. Broom Court
13. Gravel Pit
14. Rush Lane

SOUTH OF AVON
15. Money Meadow
16. Staple Hill
17. White Posts
18. Ooseland Gate (Barn)

MARLCLIFF
19. Sixteen Acres Lane
20. Cheapside
21. China Square
22. The Clink
23. Brook Leys
24. The Welshman's
25. The Nook Pool
26. The Rough (Rough Grounds)
27. Three Shires Elms

BARTON
28. Barton

BICKMARSH
29. Bickmarsh Hall
30. Clay Hall

Outlying settlements of Bidford-on-Avon

(Ordinance Survey, Gloucestershire Sheet I & III, 1924)

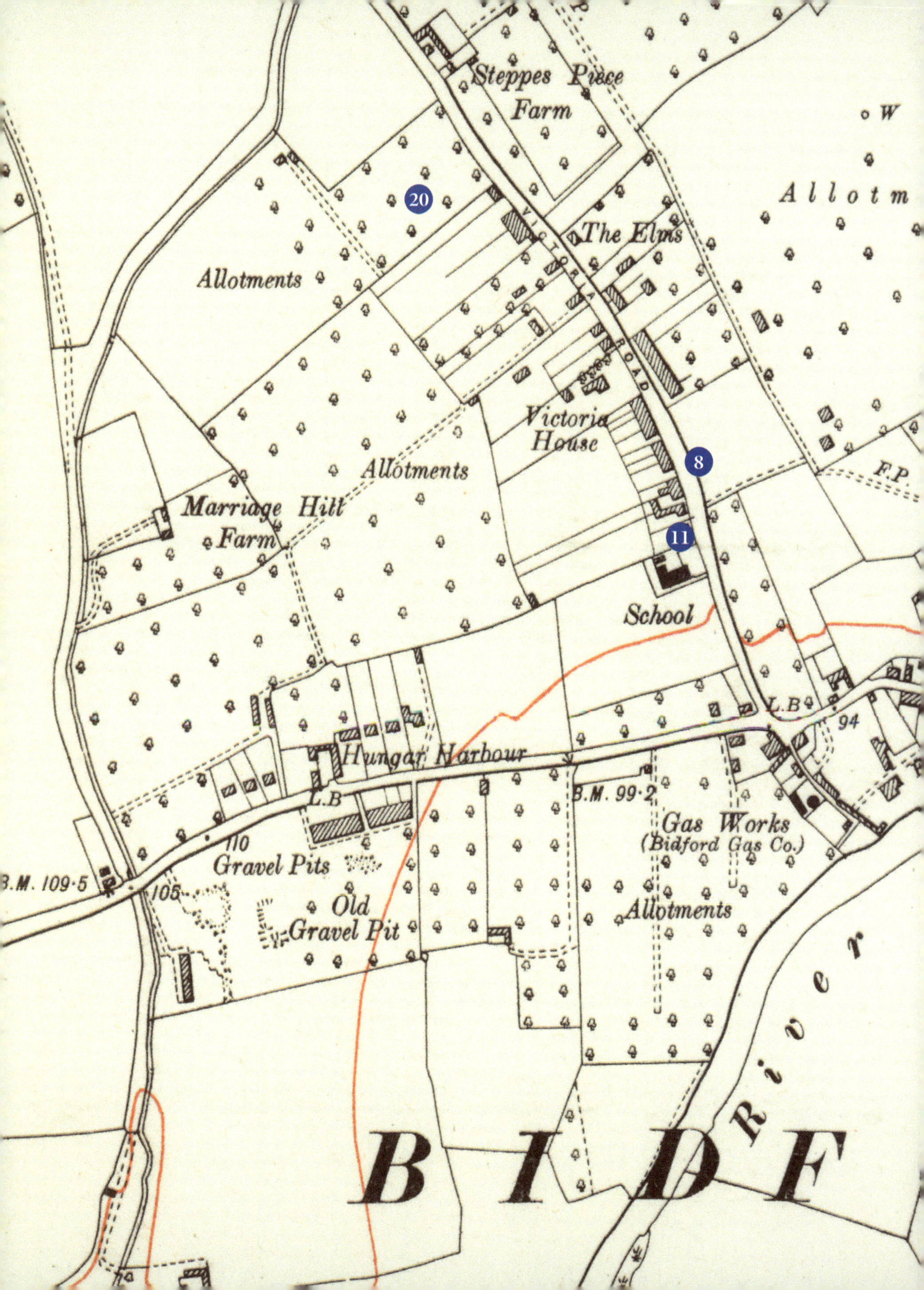
Steppes Piece
Farm
W
Allotm
20
The Elms
Allotments
VICTORIA ROAD
Victoria
House
8
F.P.
Marriage Hill
Farm
Allotments
11
School
L.B
94
Hungar Harbour
B.M. 99·2
L.B
Gas Works
(Bidford Gas Co.)
110
Gravel Pits
B.M. 109·5
105
Old
Gravel Pit
Allotments
River
BIDF

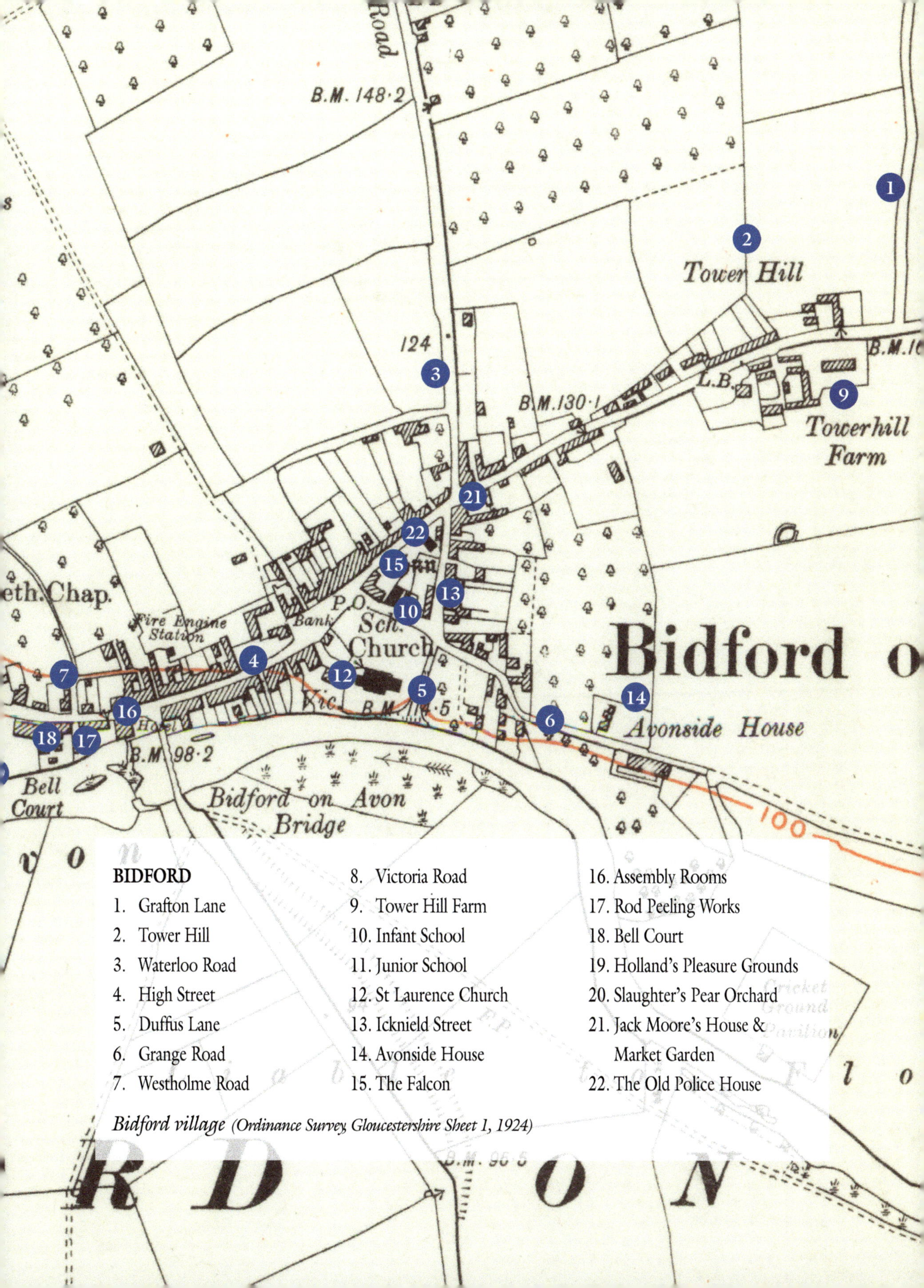

BIDFORD

1. Grafton Lane
2. Tower Hill
3. Waterloo Road
4. High Street
5. Duffus Lane
6. Grange Road
7. Westholme Road
8. Victoria Road
9. Tower Hill Farm
10. Infant School
11. Junior School
12. St Laurence Church
13. Icknield Street
14. Avonside House
15. The Falcon
16. Assembly Rooms
17. Rod Peeling Works
18. Bell Court
19. Holland's Pleasure Grounds
20. Slaughter's Pear Orchard
21. Jack Moore's House & Market Garden
22. The Old Police House

Bidford village (Ordinance Survey, Gloucestershire Sheet 1, 1924)

The original Avon Almanac from the archives of the Bidford and District History Society

Avon Almanac

A Cranhill Boy Goes to School

Strictly speaking, the Cranhill boys should have gone to Grafton School since they were just in that parish. The Bidford Parish boundary to the east is Cranhill Brook and when the 'Penny a week' schooling[1] was abolished towards the end of the 19th century, the Overseers of the Parish[2] had sufficient problems of overcrowding without having children from other parishes attending their schools.

Bidford Infant School[3], built in 1840, had a gallery section to try and cope with this problem but by 1920 there were two classes: Miss Smith[4], dressed in her dark Victorian clothes, had charge of the younger children and Miss Quail[5] was headmistress. Although a wooden screen divided the room, it must have been hard and tiring work to teach the important subjects. For arithmetic tables and the alphabet some children wrote on slates, a great economy saving on writing paper. With only two years, from the ages of five to

Church Hall, formerly Bidford Infant School.
(Photograph: Sandra Parker)

seven, before pupils moved to the 'Bottom School', repetition methods were necessary. The sonorous chanting of tables from 'twice one are two' to 'ten tens are a hundred' was repeated in a sing-song way until all but the very backward would quote them parrot fashion. The alphabet, with phonetic symbols of the letters, would also be taught by the same method and between the two it resembled opposing groups of psalm singers!

When the children had reached their seventh birthday, it was time to leave for the great strange 'Bottom School' built in 1872 in Victoria Road. Here, Mr Warner[6] was headmaster and the new arrivals were at least broken into the strange surroundings by the kind understanding of Mrs Warner who taught Standard 1. But overcrowding here was just as great a problem. There was one small classroom for Standard 1, and a room with a curtain divided 2 and 3, which can only be said to have partly separated them by sight, and not at all by sound. But the 'Big Room' was most trying for teaching because Standards 4,5,6 and 7 were here, and from the distraction caused by the conflicting sounds and babel of voices it is difficult to understand how about 200 pupils made the

Bidford Junior School (Permission of Rodney Crompton)

progress to fit them for leaving school at 14 years of age.

The school, with iron windows too high for pupils to see the outside world, was heated, if it can be called that, with an open fireplace in each room. Those unfortunates at the back of the class just shivered and any children who were sick with cold or plain hungry spent the day near the fire guard. Friday afternoons were a break from routine. The girls took needlework and always used this time before Christmas to make their Mums a small present. The boys were marched to the school gardens near Steppes Piece, unless the weather was too bad. On these occasions the whole school would crowd into the largest classroom for music and singing[7] and, later, learning and acting plays and operettas like 'Zurika'[8], 'The Men of Sherwood'[9] and similar productions. On breaking up day before Christmas each pupil was given a bar of chocolate presented by Sam G Mason[10], a school manager. Also, the School's Religious Inspector, Rev Sheard[11] of Exhall, would expound with his usual poem 'Song of the Flea'[12]. These treats were more than anticipated because those who came to school from distant cottages brought bread and jam and a bottle of cold tea or cocoa for winter dinners and usually had water to drink in the summer. This meant a relay of bottle fillers to the pump in the headmaster's yard, which was the extent of school meals and refreshment.

On winter mornings darkness ruled the early hours. Normal bedroom lighting was by candle light giving a groping glow around the room. On the other hand, candlelight, with its flame flickering in the draught, made grotesque patches on the ceiling and walls and frosted panes of the window. First occupation downstairs was washing, although a trail to the garden-end privy may have preceded this. Wise mothers in frosty weather filled a couple of pails with water overnight, thus saving a performance of burning straw around the iron pumps to thaw them out. The elm boxed lead pumps were less prone to ice up, but when filling a kettle in the dark, it was a good idea to give the handle a few jerks. Turgid black slugs used the spout for overnight somnolence, and to fill the kettle with the first water one ran the risk of the taste of boiled slug in the early cup of tea.

After a bread and lard breakfast, his hob-nailed boots sounding his footsteps, father had left for work before the rising infants, complete with tools for the day and with his food in his pail, depending on the seasons' requirements in the perpetual round of hedging, ditching, haymaking and harvest.

The observant boy now started his walk to school. Already weather wise, he noted the wind direction by the billowing black smoke from the Brickworks chimney. Wind or rain from the east lasted 24 hours at least. On the other hand, a fine day was certain if the Ragley rooks, surely the most consistent and earliest of fair weather fliers, were flying high away to the Cotswolds, instead of hanging around locally if tempest or rain was expected before their return. Usually the boys saw the 7.30 passenger train from Stratford rattling down Caly cutting[13] to Broom Junction[14], only to have a struggling start from Bidford siding[15] on its return, ***mauling*** away until Cranhill level gave it the impetus to roll and rattle down to Binton Bridge. After crossing the boundary brook, haven of holidays, the eight churches[16] would begin to come into view on a clear morning: Grafton, Exhall, Wixford, Welford, Cleeve, Salford, Bidford and Tredington Spire, with the sentinel view of Primrose Castle[17] thrown in for good measure.

The winding road, before the first of its many straightenings, camberings and surfacings,

Bidford Station (Permission of Rodney Crompton)

swept round past Shakespeare's Crab[18] and California Cottage, and the nearby communal allotments. These were where the working men of the Parish, most with large families, would rent an acre of the heavy clay land to grow a piece of wheat, a *pole* or two of potatoes and a couple of rows of plums, *'Victoria'*, *'Pershore Egg'*, and that handsome plum, *'Warwickshire Drooper'*, which would only succeed in the immediate area. The boy would see that the land was worked by hand. The two *tined* 'caly' fork would be rolling over clods of clay, sometimes in moonlight digging sessions, for it was important to set the clay up before the frost, and a sparing covering of soot would *lax it down* in the spring as fine as brown sugar. There would be each man's small rick in the centre yard ready for a communal *threshing* operation and *winnowing* in the great stone barn.

Perhaps the boy would meet up with those from Grange farm cottages, usually along the road coming out near the old stone quarry worked by Jesse Houghton[19]. The locals claimed this road as a right of way because of a traditional belief that when a corpse had been along it that made it a public road. The Grange children would take the 'Middle Road'. This route was ancient and the site of the original 'Shakespeare's Crab'. It was reckoned that each variety in a hedge dated it by 100 years. The slow growing oak and

Shakespeare's 'Crab' (Permission of Shakespeare Birthplace Trust)

Avonside House (Warwickshire County Record Office PH239/43)

ash and the hawthorn *butts*, which were swollen and heavy from perpetual hedge layering, were living examples, growing hardy on this the highest nob in the parish, which was a choice location, with its extensive views from the Royal Observer Post in World War II. The boy's father has shown him the curse of Grange high fields, *Crow Onions*, the cause of a tenant farmer swiftly changing from milk production with its tell-tale smell of onions in the churns.

Another short way to school from Grange was along the River Meadow footpath and out to 'Avonside', not so popular after an unfortunate parishioner had cut his throat under the great pear tree on Sinfoil Bank[20]. The superb gardens and lawns of Avonside had been planned and set out by Mrs Crawford[21], the Doctor's wife, with the help of John Cole[22], her gardener, and Edwin Sheasby[23], an expert dry stone walling mason. Some plants and shrubs which liked the soil conditions near the river bank were brought over from her native Ireland, and with the masses of daffodil and narcissi bulbs have matured into a splendid wild garden. She also bought the Cleeve Cider Mill when it was demolished and had it re-erected in the grounds.

Avonside was used as an emergency maternity home[24] during the Second World War. Mrs Crawford, having built a pleasant stone house at the garden's end, named it the 'Cockpit'. This house is probably the last in the district to be built in traditional stone and a great search was made for old buildings built in blue lias[25] and old hand-made tiles for re-use. The sweeping lawns down to the Avon's bank were surely a quiet resting place for the ashes of a well-beloved country Doctor[26].

But the boys of the village were more interested in the mouth-watering *espalier* French pears, wall peaches and cherries. One escapade was a waste of time. After a careful study of the high east wall siding the footpath to the Cricket Meadow for climbing holds, they found the cherries in that area to be bitter *morellos* and at least one trespasser was unable to return over the wall before an irate Cole appeared. The footpath was well used by many people of the parish using the popular, but sometimes fatal, swimming place at the 'Bend' just above the Avonside boundary.

The boy had heard that the site of the 'Cockpit' was originally a *sawpit* and wood yard jetty in the heyday of Avon navigation, next door to Burdett's Coal Wharf[27]. A lad had fallen into the swirling current here and his body was not found for many weeks until an old village woman had suggested dragging an area where several swans were swimming round and round. This was a usual place for swimming fatalities, the groping roots of pollarded *withies* and under-swept holes of the Avon very often holding down their victims for weeks on end.

1946 advertisement for Hercules bicycles.
(Alamy Stock Photo - 2F2TYWA)

The boy on his trail to school along Grange Road may have met drayman Tom Taylor[28] and the railway parcel delivery wagon with a load of cycle frames which had been consigned to Bidford Sidings. These were for the in-between house, now occupied by Mr J Styles[29], but in those days the home of the Crane brothers[30], owners later of the Hercules cycle empire, the outcome of a mini Bidford workshop.

It was difficult for the boy to pass Longford's

farm[31] without a squint at the great Tangye Gas Engine[32], used for driving farm machinery, *chaff-cutting*, root chopping and log sawing. The excitement of its steady exhaust note, 'tump, tump', was only matched by watching the immense fly-wheel and its attendant *governors* and long shuttling crankshaft, throbbing the very earth with vibrating power.

He would see the cows being turned out after hand milking into the close fields surrounding the house, which was protected and still is by a sunken 'ha ha' ditch, almost like a dry moat, which allowed grazing without fences obstructing the view from the master's house. In the yard stood a churn on a two-wheeled hand cart, emblazoned with polished brass plate inscribed 'H.Odell'[33], ready for its owner to start village deliveries with hanging oval milk buckets each of which had its attached cup measures inside.

Another hindrance to the young man's journey would be to watch the cattle drover on Stratford Market Day. A couple of men would be driving a score of fattened *steers*, taking over the complete road and grass verges. The younger drover would be hurrying away to the *foremost*, blocking off the side roads and shutting gates to prevent a melee of capering

Dredging Engines, Salford Priors

(Warwickshire County Record Office / Bomford and Evershed PH219/33)

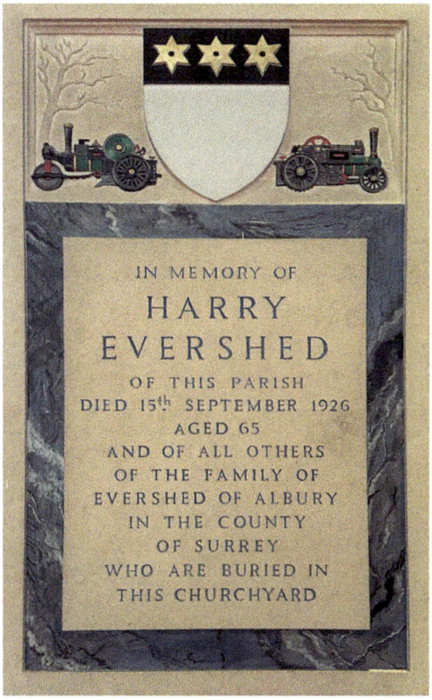

cattle breaking away from the organised bunch. Pandemonium would be sure if they were unfortunate enough to meet a Foden Steam Brewery Wagon[34] or a Sentinel truck[35] from Broom Mill. Their hissing steam safety valves as they stood by were guaranteed to make at least one group of Bidford scholars late for school. The only other traffic on the road would be Gilbert Boshier's[36] new red open top Talbot, or Dr Crawford's big yellow Sunbeam, excepting on rare occasions Cox's timber wagon, with three or four horses in harness shining with brass buckles and sweeping *hames* with shining tips. The boys knew that the woodmen and the wagoners made short work of loading large trees. After pulling alongside the trunk, the horses would be *shut off* and a couple of heavy loading *baulks* set at a sloping angle against the wagon centre pole which had adjustment holes and pegs to lengthen or shorten the wheelbase. A couple of *grouts* would be dug under the tree trunk and then a length of chain would be wound round the tree twice, with one end anchored to ground, and the chain passed over the wagon to a waiting horse at each end. A complete and steady pull rolled the trunk on to the lay bed and it was very necessary, if a nasty accident was to be avoided, to use experienced and trained *trace horses*, who knew the ways of men, otherwise any halting would result in a backward roll of trees and snatch back off the lugging horse.

A periodic highway spectacle would be steam rollers and dredging engine gangs from Bomford and Evershed[37], with their attached living van, water cart and trailers of required gear. These sets of tackle moved to contracts in many distant parts of the county and might stay away for a couple of years or more in large undertakings. The roller works at Salford also employed many local men and the owner, Willie Evershed, was a great inventor of machines and apparatus for steam work in its greatest days, and on his memorial in Salford Church is carved some of this equipment. The passing of an Evershed Roller made a vast difference to the road surface which was maintained by

Evershed memorial in St. Matthew's Chuch, Salford Priors *(Photo: Mark Shaddick)*

yearly tar spraying. Every few years however the roads needed more drastic treatment. Two inch slag from the Black Country furnaces was collected by horse and cart from Bidford siding, spread about three inches deep and then covered with fine soil from the verges and watered in before heavy rolling. Our traffic-ridden roads show this lower stratum of foundation whenever service trenching exposes these bygone methods. The tar pot was horse-drawn with a front collecting sump on which the barrels of tar were to gurgle out through the bung hole. This was heated by a side-mounted coal fire-grate. The molten tar was then pumped up into a rear header tank to be fed down hoses to two wide brooms and swept onto the road surface. Cart loads of chippings would then be spread by men with shovels with a swinging flick which resulted in an even-covered surface followed by the inevitable Aveling and Porter 7 ton Steam Roller[38] with large brass plate cut away into the shape of a prancing horse.

Tower Hill, because of its busy horse traffic, would miss the tarring operation. Potholes were filled, and it was heavily rolled to give the horses a chance to set in their shod hooves when lugging a heavy load. But when descending, *skid pans* would be fixed to the

Bomford and Evershed Steam Roller.
(Permission of the Operations Director Bomford Turner Limited)

rear wheels. This slick surface made an ideal place to set a spinning top whipped down the main street on the way to school, depending on the season. Large iron hoops would also run down the village and be left at school for the return homeward in the evening.

The Sleepy Village

Although the village appeared from the high surrounding ground to be sleepy and peaceful, it was a hive of activity to anyone strolling down Tower Hill. Percy Bryan[39] would be busy mixing colours in his sign-writer's shop and practising his clever art of reverse printing on glass with gold leaf, but an unshipped Churchill tank[40] put paid to this shed. His father, John Bryan[41], would be loading his builder's hand carts with ladders and building materials to be pushed by a couple of tradesmen and boy to some distant site or nearby repair job. Lower down, Harry Wilkes[42] would be bringing in his cows from pasture into his dairy and the girls, after milking, would be getting the milk float ready for village deliveries. Also Fosbroke's[43] milkman, A Ash[44], would be on his daily journey with cans on yoke from Salford Road with the house milk. Jeweller Smith[45] would be ticklin away in his Watch and Clock Repair Shop. In earlier days he was able to draw a tooth on demand, without the comfort of cocaine, of course.

There was bound to be something happening in Fred Holder's[46] rickyard[47]. Perhaps it was the men *shutting* in their horses to cart or dray for land work operations, or the hum of the threshing drum droning away with a periodic groan as the feeding man or woman in *herden* apron on top of the shaking box pushed in the broken sheafs, thrown over to him and cut in mid-air by the bondsman. Although the corn ricks were built up on *staddle* stones to protect them from rat damage, these varmints found a way in. A surround of three foot high rabbit wire would

Pictured Right: An example of staddle stones

(Shutterstock - 2159652557)

be pegged round the rick being thrashed. This was monitored inside by busy boys with short clubbing sticks hoping to show a top score of rats killed by the end of the day. It was always a source of wonderment to watch the engineer set his steam traction engine dead level and perfectly square with the box so that the fifty foot flagging driving belt ran true on the large fly wheel. Once set, out came a bucket from the driving platform and the belt would be smeared with sticky 'Black Jack' dressing with a resulting rear and jostle of the box as the power took hold and the engine settled down to a steady throb. The attendant men would have to keep pace with operations: the bolting men carrying away straw high on *shuppick forks* to the nearby growing straw rick; the bag man moving away his sacks and careful not to let them overfill with corn from the *rolling flutes*, and weighing off on his heavy wooden scales; and the *rowing man* clearing away *chaff* from under the shaking sieve frames and humping them in a large sheet, shoulder high to the crew yard for treading in by cattle, after seeing that this chaff house was full for winter feed. At the end of the day the 280 lb sacks would be loaded by two men with a short pole between them, thus easing the pitching up of these weighty bags onto the wagon bed.

Nearby was the Police Station. In these pre-Panda days, Copper Munday[48] roamed round his beat and made his points by cycle, although for private use he sported a belt drive twin Douglas motor cycle combination with basket work sidecar. Point duty was not among his operations but to be seen about the village no doubt made many would-be mischief makers wary of the consequences of their misdeeds.

Opposite the Police Station was Henry Cowper's[49] coal yard. His heavy *drays* were fitted with front shaft boards to prevent sacks of coal shooting forward on to an unfortunate horse and to contain the many varied parcels and packages he carried as Railway Agent for Bidford Siding and Broom Junction. A regular load programme was Manchester flour to the Co-Op and coal to the Gas Works.

The Police House *(Photograph: Sandra Parker)*

Handy next door was Charles Dowdeswell[50] the saddler. Behind his small-paned window he worked away at his bench making collars and cart saddles and pony harness for the spring cart users. Hung round the shop were sets of harness, iron carthorse *ridgehorse chains*, belly bands, *cruppers*, leather *traces* and reins of cut leather and rope, *G.O. lines* for the plough teams, fancy bridles with bright silver bits and over all the smell of soaking *leather bends* and *ratted* and wax thread ends. Come summer he would display knitted ear muffs to keep away the tormenting flies, although some carters swore by a sprig of alder in the bridle for this purpose. He had a special shelf of horse appendages: *Curry Combs* and *Dandy Brushes*, bottles of *Cure All Five Oils*, *Neatsfoot oil* to keep harness supple, and mane dressing ribbons for the more sophisticated horseman to match his own horse brasses and *martingales.*

The next house was the abode of Dr Hobbes[51] and young Crawford. With its tiny waiting room most folk sat on the steps outside, from where Dr Hobbes could be seen in his small dispensary with rows of strange and important looking jars each with its emblazoned description of contents. He had a favourite saying that 'Pea picking was a cure for all ills', because many ailments and afflictions had to be endured till after this important labour, necessary to shoe and clothe the family before winter set in, was completed. In his early days of

1887 Jubilee Plate showing the Falcon Inn
(Permission of Mark Shaddick)

practice in Bidford he did his rounds on horseback to the outlying hamlets complete with special instrument case for many on the spot surgical operations. Later a horse and dogcart was more convenient until Dr Crawford came with a large open yellow Sunbeam car.

Opposite the Falcon[52], which had been made into six tenements after its disuse in 1840 as village workhouse, stood Walter Smith's bakery, now at the rear, with stabling and shed, after an earlier cellar bakehouse used by the Rose family. Beyond Harry Odell's dairy and rear sited tea room for the weekend use of Birmingham visitors, was the Post Office with Pa Collins[53] as Postmaster. No side-lines were evident here. It housed the only telephone box in the village and a small exchange board was mounted in a rear room. This necessitated an urgent trip to 'put somebody through' in between serving stamps, franking letters or serving in the adjacent stationery department. It was a useful fount of knowledge for the village grapevine news system because any outgoing telegram messages could be heard by locals waiting for service in the front shop.

Every morning at the next door Bull's Head old Mrs Spiers[54], the landlady, could be seen twirling her mop, making sure that her section of pavement was clean after mopping and *hearthstoning* her own flagstones. Perhaps she would glance into the neighbouring Sill's 'Top Shop'. This was the crockery shop where many Bidford Jubilee 1887 plates were sold, now rare, as are pottery models of the Falcon. The shop was later taken over by Noakes and Crofts[55], and its proprietor Jimmy Parker made it into a music room and theatre for his masterly hobby of puppet making and showing. Past the bank was Bidford's only paper shop. William Jones[56], who had married Miss Farr and took on the business, could be seen careering out of his back entrance through Boshier's yard on his round tank BSA and sidecar to meet the 7.55am Birmingham train to Broom to collect the village papers and periodicals. His nickname, 'Skipper', stems from his other important occupation, that of Steamer and Boat man at Holland's, and few must have known better than he how the bed of the river varied between Bidford and Cleeve Prior. He would have had invaluable information to give during the present dredging operations at Marlcliff to open up the river again for boating. 'Skipper' Jones was only in distress once. He left Cleeve Mill with Steamer and Trailer Boat crammed with Brummy day trippers. Close to the Arrow mouth the trailer boat sprang a leak and although women and children were seated on the *gunwales*, the 'Skipper' took no notice of their yells for help. The resourceful Jones, however, was making full steam ahead to beach her

The Old Falcon Inn- opposite the Bull's Head *(Permission of Mark Shaddick)*

The Bull's Head Inn *(Permission of Rodney Crompton)*

The Fisherman's Rest (Permission of Rodney Crompton)

The White Lion Hotel and Mason's Arms (Permission of Rodney Crompton)

on the Marlcliff shelf where the irate occupants clambered ashore under the hills.

Across the green bank, before the War Memorial[57] was erected and surrounded by superb crazy stone terracing by Fred Houghton, was the Fisherman's Rest[58], whose landlord, Bill Gardner, made great industry with river works. Next door was Brighton House, Mrs Edmunds' sweet shop[59] with, as a neighbour, John Gould[60], the 'Working Man's Butcher'. Whatever conditions were available for slaughtering at the rear must have been matched by the normal practice of Butchers' shops in Bidford, namely, an open shop with meat hung for display, exposed to the dusty rigours of the Main Road. It is true that Tom Taylor, the roadman, with broom and handcart covered his length daily, but after his labours horse traffic left that which 'was all over Bidford', although boys with trucks and buckets made their pocket money collecting this end product for rose growers. Edward Sill's[61] large rose garden, destroyed when the Jubilee Hall[62] was built, was the reason why Ernest Wilkes's[63] house was named 'Rose View'. Hemming Lane, his backway, and also that of Jim Kendall's,[64] the bespoke shoemaker, was busy with wagonettes and coach hire to the stations, charging one shilling per load of passengers and no charge for waiting time. There was a choice of Brougham[65] with glass window cab and centre doors, Landau[66] with simple hood for protection, or open wagonette, which some fathers would hire for the day on Bank Holidays for a family picnic in the Cotswolds.

Cars were now numbering half a dozen in Bidford. For hire, however, the fashionable taxi was Gilbert Boshier's red open Lanchester[67], but John Evans'[68] Calthorpe[69] was evident also. The Co-op shops[70] with their front for horses' entry made for busy traffic opposite Jimmy Elsmore's General Shop[71], which was a calling place for tramps. A man leaving Stratford Workhouse would be given a cheque entitling him to a bit of bread and cheese before making for the Evesham Grubber[72]. Next door was Tinker Wilcox[73], gunsmith, and, as his nickname suggests, an expert in

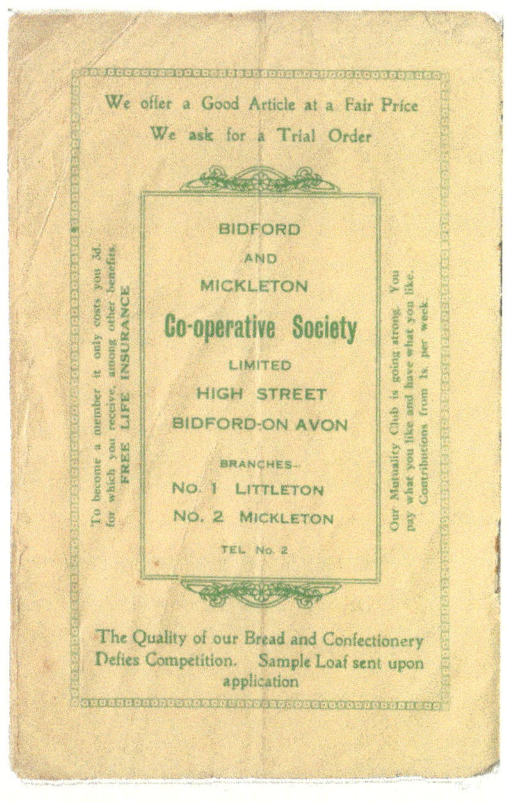

An advert for the Co-operative Society in the Bidford Improvements Association Horse Races and Sports Carnival Official Programme, Thursday 9th August 1928. Bidford Improvements Association, 1928

tin smithing and locks and keys, his shop littered with gun cartridges, yokes etc. It is rumoured that after a house sale, furniture with locked doors and drawers would have to receive his attention after a mysterious absence of keys to fit them.

After John Davis's bakery[74] with side flue oven, and Gray and Friend's great draper's emporium[75], was the slaughter house of George Winnett[76]. This was the mecca of inquisitive boys. On Monday morning the beasts for slaughter would be driven up the village and if the usual method of holding hurdles across the road failed to coax the unfortunate victim into the *laird* pens for starving ready for Tuesday's killing, another method had to be resorted to. The rear slaughter room with felling ring and block housed a large wooden wheel in the roof and strong rope, which passed through a ring in the floor and was attached to the beast's neck. This resulted in the animal being slowly and surely pulled in from the street or pen and the head trapped by the ring to the floor. A wary butcher then dodged the flaying legs to straddle the neck and drive a pole axe between the eyes before quickly sticking and bleeding, and boys would catch the blood in a bucket and stir until set for black puddings. Sheep were the most pathetic, their wide set knowing eyes waiting for the knife thrust to despatch them, and it was the kindest law of the century when humane killers were made compulsory. Opposite the slaughter house another butcher, Mr F J Prickett[77], had his shop with rear entry passages, and women queued here in the First War to have their ration stamps torn out of their family ration books.

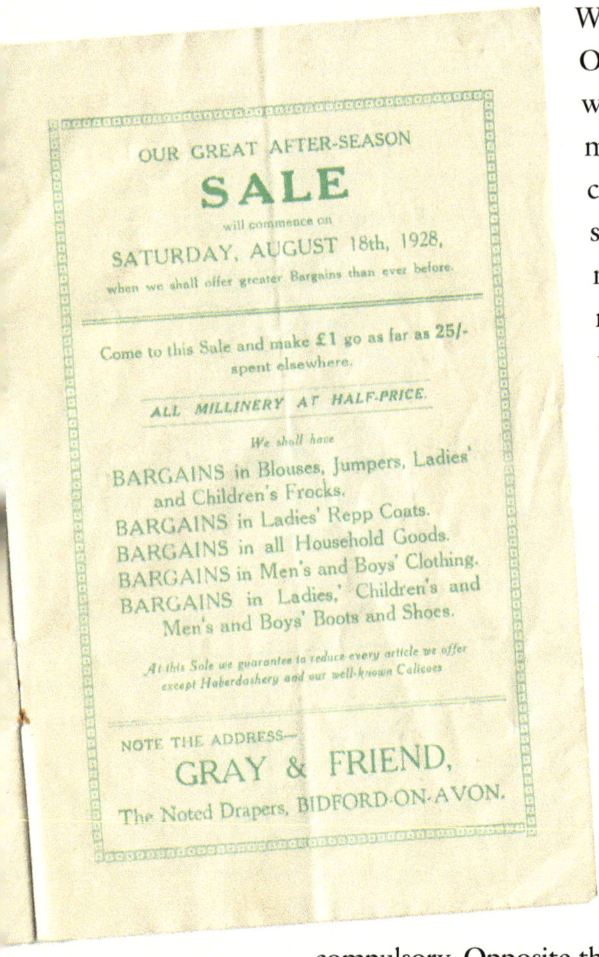

An advert for Gray and Friend in the Bidford-on-Avon Improvements Association Horse Races and Sports Carnival Official Programme, Thursday 9th August 1928. Bidford Improvements Association, 1928

The nearby Mason's Arms[78], the last pub in Bidford to have its own working brewhouse complete with riveted copper boiling pans and wooden mash tub for *wort*, was a handy place of refreshment for the adjoining fire station with two-horse manual machine. Near the bridge were Barber Bennett's shops.[79] He was an expert fiddle player and the village photographer. His wall sign outside was a target for boys jumping up to touch but this was remedied by his brainwave of putting a row of gramophone needles along the bottom edge and resulted in boys arriving home with tortured torn hands secretly hidden in pockets for fear of further punishment.

Assembly Rooms.

(Permission of Rodney Crompton)

Noakes and Crofts' shops were originally E J Sill's, who besides owning the Brickworks had a Pharmacy and other side-lines. He was agent for Mr Dent[80] of Worcester, who would bring over each week blanks for leather goods and collect them after they had been sewn by women homeworkers using gloving machines.

Edward Sill built an imposing house next door and when he applied for a wine and spirits licence, the landlord of the White Lion[81] took umbrage and built a three storey block of shops and Assembly Rooms overhead to stop his view over the river and meadows. Edward opened the new brickworks following the closure of the old Marley Bank pits, to supply bricks for the tunnels and bridges on the Evesham-Ashchurch line[82], also Skilts at Gorcott[83]. These were taken by Steam Engine and trailers.

Another industry was William Gardner's rod peeling works[84] adjoining the Assembly Rooms. He owned several *osiernates* above the bridge and at Barton. The osiers, after being carefully hoed and kept clear of weeds,

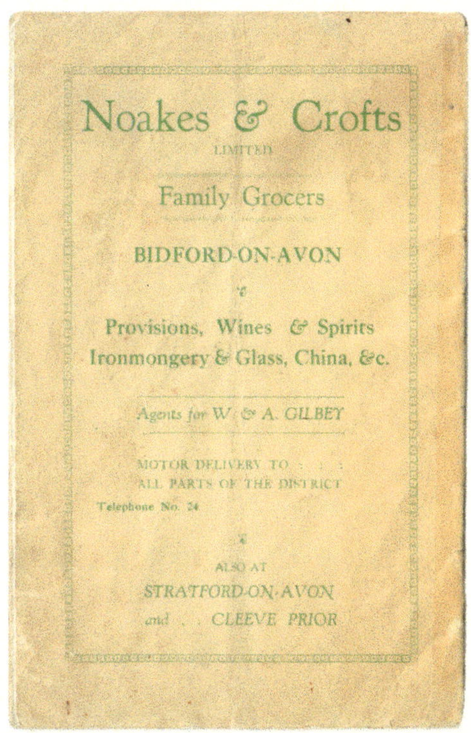

An advert for Noakes & Crofts in the Bidford Improvements Association Horse Races and Sports Carnival Official Programme, Thursday 9th August 1928. Bidford Improvements Association, 1928

would be cut in July and then floated down the river on large pontoons about 20 feet long and 4 feet beam. Incidentally, these were also used to recover the many bodies of drowned holiday trippers who did not believe the Avon was treacherous with holes and deep underpull currents. The *withies* arriving at the locks nearby would then be peeled by women pulling them through V prongs, although those used for plum *pot hampers* (40 lbs) and round sieves (20 lbs) would be woven in the bark.

Mention of the locks one is reminded of Arthur Denness[85], landlord of the White Lion, and his garage under the Assembly Rooms, a home of Titan tractors. He also had a scheme to use the flow of the river for electricity generating. This was probably shelved because of the difficulty of sending D.C. current underground, although there was great opposition from the Gas Works shareholders.

Nearby Bell Court[86] was the home of the Bailey family and the present Mrs Sweetzer's shop was the engine generating room with large twin cylinder Crossley Gas Engine[87]

High Street, Bidford-on-Avon (Cowper's Series 6) (Permission of Rodney Crompton)

Holland's River Tea Garden and The River *(Permission of Rodney Crompton)*

with its unusual two stroke exhaust. A small tobacconist's shop of Mrs Lea[88] advertising 'Guinea Gold' and Woodbine cigarettes at five for twopence was on the corner of Westholme Road. Here grew some large elms by a spring which swept out into the road and quite often flooded the bottom of the village road which was then close to Kemble Cottage. This gave the earlier name of Victoria Road as 'Dampus Lane' and was a cast iron excuse for non-attendance at School: 'Couldn't get through, sir'.

Holland's Pleasure Grounds and Steamers[89] were crowded every weekend and holidays with cheap trip passengers from Birmingham to Broom Junction. Some organisations such as Birmingham Police brought their own band and played near the tea rooms, which was originally a sanatorium building from Shipston.

SPRING

A Bickmarsh Boy goes to School

The men who were employed on the Bickmarsh and Barton farms had large families in the early 1920s. Upwards of 60 children came over the bridge to school. Some came from as far as the 'Rough' along the Honeybourne Road, and these numbers were increased with people from Clay Hall, Brookleys, China Square, Cheapside, Sixteens Lane, The Clink, Barton Barn and Crooked Corner.

The Bickmarsh boys knew the 'Nook Pool', lately filled in and the land added to the Gliding Club grounds and runway. It was one of the original quarries among several at Bickmarsh and was very deep. It was known that a steam pumping engine was on the bottom shelf. The quarrymen were having dinner when a deep underground spring gushed out and the men quickly left their work and always afterwards the pool was brim full of water even in a drought period. The boys would be watching travelling engines and threshing tackle outfits pull up at this watering place by the roadside. There were many horses and several wagons on Bickmarsh Farm but Blackwells[90] had a couple of sets of steam ploughing tackle for the heavy clay land and no doubt the boys had a fine time with these old codgers and the long trail to school hindered by their operations. Another delay would be violet and primrose gathering from the quarry banks that made a drab, high windowed classroom gay with flowers.

It was time for wheat rolling with two-horse flat rolls leaving long marks across the fields with a reverse mark on the return *bout*, but the young wheat soon rose again for the wind to sweep across in billows. Coming down Staple Hill, however, the boys would be among the smallholders' allotments. The lighter land was usually worked with a one horse digger 'Planet' plough[91] with attendant *dray* and other implements, perhaps a set of *chain harrows* to use after pea drilling; and waiting for the sun-warmed 'ground to steam' before beet drilling and before setting up the inevitable *'mawkins'* for bird scaring. They would see the women in white bonnets and aprons picking *gillies*, radish bunching and spring onion pulling. The allotment piece 'Catsmere' was used for the tipping of weekly parish 'night soil', collected by horse tankers into a slurry pit surrounded by ashes, and when the wind was roadwards, this caused many to hurry past the encountering smell.

The Bickmarsh boys would meet up with Barton and Marlcliff people at the cross roads and in time of spring floods, wagons would be at Ooseland Gate to take them through the flood. They had already been ferried from their homes at Barton in punts or flat bottom boats. As soon as the Avon became bank high it would take a short cut through Ooseland to Marlcliff. Although the raising of the road at the White Posts did improve matters, it caused quite a dangerous current of water to sweep through the gates and over and through the hedges, leaving them hurdle-like with debris from the river banks.

Boats on the Avon *(Permission of Rodney Crompton)*

After flooding, weeds soon became abundant in the Gardners' *osiernates* opposite the Church and Duffus Lane[92] and the boys would notice the men busy *hooving* amongst the osiers to keep the resultant rods straight and clean.

When the boys reached the age of 14 years, it was time to go on to the farm with their elders, perhaps as plough boy, or that lonely day-long job of bird minding, although this was a grand opportunity for some excellent catapult practice, digging out a rabbit or two or setting wires overnight.

Some boys with a bit of time in hand would make a detour on the way to school along Holland's entry and out at The Pleck near the gas works. One reason for this was so that they could watch Holland's bringing out their *carvel built* double scullers, mahogany punts and Canadian birch canoes into the morning sun and setting them upside down on trestles for the annual varnishing. But a more important reason was to note the condition of a very useful row of *'Worcester'* and *Blenheim'* apple and *'William'* pear trees planted conveniently against the footpath wall, because every gardener knows 'that if they be thinned it makes for better fruit'. Holland's entry, 100 yards long and close-walled, was very useful for a local to wager a bet in the pubs amongst Brummies who had not 'brought their mug into the country with them'. The plan was to take on all comers for a hundred yards sprint providing that the Bidford man could choose the track and have one yard's start. Holland's entry made it impossible for a runner to pass the front man, and much free ale was quaffed when money was otherwise tight!

A Blenheim Orange
Wilhelm Lauche, Deutsche Pomologie.
(Wikimedia Commons)

The Broom Schoolboy in Spring

The Broom boys left for school leaving the great hum of the Roller Mills[93] churning out flour and animal feed, driven by the rushing water from the rear pound or in times of drought by the huge diesel engine. Broom Junction was busy with passenger goods trains, and an interesting hindrance was the turntable to return the Stratford trains back again through Bidford siding. Some perhaps met the paper train from Birmingham for delivery on the way to school, and they may have seen the platelayer gang set up their two axle bogie before they trudged off with their tools to 'Caly Cutting' in time for lunch or in earlier days the 'Four Alls'[94]. At this time the boys might detour down Rush Lane alongside the new school boundary[95] but this ancient right of way is now grubbed and

Broom Junction *(Permission of Rodney Crompton)*

ploughed. Some say this was a way to Salford before the Marriage Hill [96] road and the new Arrow Bridge. The line continued across the main road and along the river meadows to cross the Arrow at the Gravel Shallows in line with the beacon tower on Salford Church.

The orchards of Steppes Piece would be showing the first blossom. The going would be difficult if Parker's ditch was in flood. In fact when the houses were half-built in May 1931, water ran through them and a flat bottomed boat was kept handy. And due to a mistake in drain surveying near the Junior School the Steppes Piece drain pipes were laid with two courses of brick under each joint and soil from Broom Gravel Pit, brought by horse and cart, to cover them over. Over the hedge in the Park they would see the labourers wheat *hooving*, because this was in the days before selective weedkiller killed foes and friendly tender plants alike. The farmers walking over their work would be careful in crossing the centre area because some pieceworkers had been known to hoove well round the outside and then take the plates out in the middle for an hour or so.

Some boys reported to school with large iron hoops made from three-quarter inch circular

The Jam Factory, Broom, J.E. Williams 1977 *(Permission of the Broom Research Group)*

'Bother'em Dick (ladies unknown)
(Permission of Bob Marshall)

rod. These were the rims of seed drills and had probably been scrounged from among the debris round Broom jam factory [97] cast out of Harry Mason's [98] blacksmith's shop scrap. They seemed to be able to supply most of the school's requirements in this line.

A few would detour along the Westholme Road footpath between narrow high hedges and come out at Victoria Road stile. Perhaps they would see 'Bother'em Dick,[99] the well sinker, on his way to some job. It was said with jest that the 'first time he went up a ladder was down a well', but having dug a well at Grafton to about 70 feet, he refused payment because he had not found water. Also, that while digging a well at Salford he asked a neighbour for hot water for his tea can. On being refused, he told the neighbour to padlock the water in his own well and side tracked the spring at a greater depth, thus emptying the other well. On another occasion he was digging a new householder's well in Westholme Road and refused to come up at dinner time for the chain and bucket assistant to pay his usual visit to the Pleasure Boat [100]. Hoping to last out this period without assistance, he was found on his mate's return stood on shovels and board, shouting for help!

The observant boy would notice a new-fangled apparatus to light Broom Hall [101] with gas. A large weight was lifted on poles with pulley blocks and its gradual descent exerted

Broom Hall
(Warwickshire County Record Office PH21/62)

pressure which forced acetylene mixture through the feed pipes.

At this time the four-man platelayer gang would be scything the track banks and sloping the sides which required a queer and awkward stance to sweep their tools upwards while standing odd-legged among the grass and briars. Over the wire fence, built from old sleepers sawn square, a gardener with a *piece* in Spreading Oak would be grafting stock by the old method of raffia tie and cow dung and clay daubing, always remembering to lick the sharply cut *scions* before fixing to coax the slivers of bark to knit together.

Avon Almanac

SUMMER

The Cranhill Boy in Summer

Around Cranhill and Caly Cutting was a piece of discovery and wonder. He would sit by the track to see the passenger and goods engine slowly climbing the incline and have a wave from the crew. Perhaps he had put a couple of pins crossways on the track which formed themselves into the shape of a pair of fairy scissors after the trucks had passed over them. Summer Hill farm was in the depressed state of *'Dog and Stick'* farming and the small copses of sloe and blackthorn and briars would be the home of many varieties of birds and ground animals. These peaceful surroundings seemed miles away from the village and there was the parish boundary brook to explore from mouth to source as it rippled away over the blue lias stones under the railway culvert built for it. It was usual to set off for the day with bread and jam sandwiches and build *stanks* and waterfalls and make tadpole pools. The irony of these days was that one of the explorers [102] ended his days on the Burma railway built in the Japanese war. The banks were a haven for grass snakes and glinting kingfishers and goldfinch feeding in groups on the numerous thistle heads. The gypsies knew that this was an area of *teasels* for Christmas decorations but the secret places of the wild orchid were only known to a few. After the boys had helped to burn off the embankments the ground would be littered with small stiff snakes among the smouldering undergrowth. But come a thunderstorm and there would be a sudden transformation of virgin grass, helped it is said, by the potash from the wood ash.

But school days had to be endured between visits and the boy may have met Elijah Bryan,[103] the carrier to Stratford and Evesham with horse and *dray* and small growers' produce for market, returning with empties of *pot hampers* and sieves and the numerous small shopping parcels he had been commissioned to collect.

Money Meadow *(Permission of Rodney Crompton)*

On a very rare occasion, he may have met the covered wagon emblazoned 'Atora Beef Suet', drawn by a pair of oxen shod with double split shoes to protect their hooves, and the circus may be coming for its one night stand in the Money Meadow[104] complete with elephants and horse-drawn animal cages, gaudy caravans and all the paraphernalia of these 'get up and move' people.

Haymaking was now afoot and over the hedge a two-horse mower would be cutting away, its triangular blades sliding through the glistening fingers making short work of the swaying grass which fell away from the long *swatheboard*, making a clean sweep for the next cut. The busy blade was only hindered when an early corner was reached and the metallic click of the driving wheel *ratchet* was heard, although the horseman with his eye on acreage would soon run off the corners round to save halting for a square turn. The horses had been carefully paired. They were chosen and kept for mowing by picking out a pair striding forward with even step, which kept the *swingletree* in a steady square pull, as opposed to the heavy horse plough team who, whether they were fillers or foremost and in land or furrow, stepped out at their natural distance to the *headland* ('Haddledum')

Haymaking Marriage Meadows *(Warwickshire County Record Office PH21/61)*

where they turned themselves by a quiet command of the ploughman, 'come back' or 'go back', to cross the land and straighten up into the next furrow. This was controlled by the wise *foremost* but the great heavy shire *fillers* had the task of lugging out the last few feet of run before the plough was laid aside on the *shell-board* for coming back and going round.

Mowing was all very well until a mouse nest or two blocked up the knife which meant that the horses had to lug back the mower by its centre pole attached to the collar hooks, there being no *backband* on the harness. Sometimes a partridge nest would be encountered and more often than not, the mother would limp away pretending she had a broken wing while the brood scattered in all directions. In the corner of the field, a tripod bench would be set up for the helper to bolt a spare blade on to be sharpened with a reaper file. It was a moment's work to slip this spare in when the outfit was passing by.

After a day or two, depending on the weather condition, the one horse swathe turner would turn each cut of hay into *walleys*, and then, sunshine being kind, the hay rake would move down and bring the hay into *cocks*. It was a dangerous machine with large iron tyred wheels, and was cleared to empty by a hand or foot lever. Since the operator was riding forward, the resulting clank, or a horse, frightened perhaps by a wasp's nest, meant that he could easily fall into the machine and be dragged across the field. The mowing times were usually the same as the ploughmen's i.e. begin at 7 o'clock, lunch at 10 and work through till 3.30pm unless the weather was good and spare horses were brought in.

Wagons now came on to the field to carry the hay, with forward and rear *shrove ladders* to increase the load. The hay was cleared up by *shuppick* or *pikle fork* on to the load making sure to build round in courses for a safe load and easier pitching on to the rick in the corner of the field. If they had taken a chance and carried too quickly, the rick would give off early morning steam or perhaps even fire from spontaneous combustion, although some sprinkled salt in layers to help prevent this happening. It was now left for the thatcher and later cutting, a skilful operation with off-set handled hay knife and *trussing machine* standing by.

Grafton Lane would now be reached and it was before the first council houses in Bidford had been built. It was little more than a cart track to the fields of Longford's farm and Summer Hill was only passable by pulling aside the encroaching briars and bushes from the deep muddy clay track, used as a major hazard for early motor cycles in the Colmore Cup Trials.[105] On a warm summer night the sun-warmed sleepers of the railway track would glisten with masses of glow-worms, so much so that the fire brigade was called out because someone passed by and thought the sleepers were embering with ghostly fire.

If it was Ascension Day, the schoolchildren would march up to Church and after the service disperse at the Lych Gate and be at a loose end for the rest of the day. Perhaps they would see old John Collett,[106] the gravedigger, at his periodic task who said that 'a foot spread on the top was easier than digging a foot out of the bottom', or they would meet up with the returning milking cows being driven round Grange[107] to Summer Meadow grazing. Their resultant road fouling did not improve the lot of the patients trailing round to Dr Crawford's surgery at Avonside.

Tiger Tim's Weekly *(Permission of Bob Marshall)*

But maybe they were due for a haircut at Tommy Hope's[108] in his barber's shop at the Falcon: the one large room seemed to be sufficient for all things with a perpetually laid food table near the great stone fireplace, an ancient hand-operated brush machine for wig dressing, and a gas meter in a corner cupboard which just received a hefty kick for rejuvenation when the naked lights flickered low, much to the detriment of Bidford Gas Company's finances!

It may have been though one of his Stratford days, when he cycled over to the Theatre for hair appointments, in which case boys would sit on his doorstep, reading their handed round comics such as 'Chips', 'Comic Cuts', 'Rainbow', 'Tiger Tim's Weekly' or on rare occasions, 'Boys Own Paper' and 'The Gem' with adventures of Billy Bunter and Co.[109]

Some did a recce to Icknield Street to see what was going on. The masons were always at work at Davis's,[110] the sculptors working inside the sheds and a labourer slowly cutting through blocks of Inkberrow and York stone on the *pitsaw*, and perhaps the boy would make himself useful by pouring water from a can on to the huge suspended bow saw as the block was slabbed for headstones.

The boy would be looking round for Kit, the mare and the *dray* loaded with masons' tools, headstone and curbs, ready to leave for a fixing job. To jog, trot or just dawdle along meant a pleasant day's outing to nearby Grafton or Welford churchyard. They may have had an early start, however, to Littleton or Fladbury or reflooring Tardebigge Church chancel floor.

The sheds are now the home of Warwick County Fire Brigade Station A10. It was necessary to lay new drains when alterations were made. An old retired mason's labourer stood by and watched with interest the new builders with electric tools showing their prowess and bragging about modern methods. 'Curby', however, told them they would come to a halt next day and of course he was not believed. He had noticed that the line of drain would pass directly through the *saw pit* which had been filled with granite and lias lumps of stone, and a quiet country smile of the watcher was 'giving-in time' for those modern machine capers.

He was also useful when a young mason was unable to fix a long grave slab to its sub-curb. His method was to set sugar lumps in dry cement, lower in the slab carefully and add a sprinkle of water which melted the sugar and wet the cement making everything settle into a good sound joint.

If the wheelwright was tiring, the boy was fixed up for the rest of the day. Early on the blacksmith would be making the iron tyres, heating them in the hand bellows blown forge and then hand welding the join together with sledgehammer on the ringing anvil. This was a tricky operation with urgent work needed just as the metal glowed at the correct colour, the metal afterwards dowsed in water for chilling. The blacksmith knew exactly how much to allow for shrinking on to the wooden *fellies* of a wheel by checking the inside measurement of the rim with his travelling wheel with starting chalk mark and counted revolutions.

Next door at the wheelwright's was a large circular iron platform with central hole to take a screw clamp through the hub of the wheel to hold it fast. The wheelwright, having checked the outside edge of the wheel with his *traveller* and chalk mark, now set the wheel on this platform and screwed it down tight. Meanwhile, the iron tyres had been set flat on firebricks and a wood fire lit round them till they were red with heat. When all was ready, the men, shielding their faces from the blistering heat, lifted out the tyre with *dog irons* and dropped them over the wheel. This was a moment of trust for all craftsmen concerned. The tyre was quickly cooled with cans of water standing by ready and then hammered down with *sledges* for an even fit, and as they cooled, frightening cracks were heard as the shrinking iron pulled in the ash fellies and cleft oak spokes into the wych elm hub which had been seasoning 8 or 10 years before turning.

The boy may have looked round the carpenter's shop. Perhaps a wagon or *dray* was being *rebeaded* and stood on its runners and springs on the base wheels with its accompanying ironmongery laid out for re-fixing. The iron top and bottom turnplate, screw gearing for brakes and a couple of *skid pans* on chains lay by. Another would be receiving its first coat of pink primer before final blue coat and attention by the signwriter with his many-coloured palette and steady stick with blob on the end. But the underside of the ash shafts was never painted, to allow them to continue drying out hard and not rot when an all over coat would seal the wood.

A typical wheelwright's workshop *(Shutterstock: 1802710159)*

Returning to the blacksmith who had a couple of horses for shoeing, the boy saw how each hoof in turn would be lifted up on to a tripod stand, the clenched nails of the previous shoeing prised back with a double-ended cross chisel and the nails tapped back to allow the shoe to drop off or be pulled with a large pair of pincers. The feet were then rasped level to remove hoof growth since the last shoeing and the *frog* cleaned out with the curved end knife kept for this operation.

Before taking the old shoes into the smithy, the smith would collect his traditional shaped tool box, heavy wood about 2 feet x 18 inches with cross over iron handle, higher on one end to hold nails, semi-circular cut outs in the centre for rasps and a clear bottom for pincers, hammer and knife. If the blacksmith bought ready-made shoes, he would heat them on the forge and hammer them into a shape as the cast off pattern. Otherwise, he would chop off a length of shoeing iron and start from scratch.

The new shoes being ready, they would be reheated and then picked up with a square pointed chisel driven into a nail hole. With the hoof between his legs the smith would burn on the shoe to a level fit. This caused an obnoxious smell as the foot charred away. Then after chilling, the shoe would be fixed on with nails slantwise to go through the side of the hoof and the end of the nail twisted off with the smith's claw hammer, the hoof being set on the floor for the turning over and tapping down of the remaining portion of nail end.

The smith would also make pig rings from shoeing nails. They were hammered to a long thin strip with very sharp end and pushed through the nose of the pig and rolled into a circle to stop them *routing*.

The Bickmarsh Boy in Summer

Until the county boundary adjustment, three shires met at Big Hoden field[111] and the boy knew the group of elms to mark the spot. Perhaps his family lived at the 'Rough' or 'Nook', in which case they had a Stratford doctor which meant walking a short cut through the Welshmans[112] or Dorsington to see him at Stratford. If they lived at Cheapside, they were in Worcestershire, and Evesham their town of administration, but luckier folk at Clay Hall[113] and Sixteen Acres had to come to Bidford for their medical man. Dr Crawford had a medical club enabling parents to pay a small sum each year to cover the medical requirements for the family, not that any were missed by their great conscientious doctor whether they paid or not.

Dr Crawford, pictured seated front centre with fellow surviving service men from Bidford after the first world war (We Will Remember Them. p.162)

The pea picking time was approaching and the wide Bickmarsh fields would be spread with lines of mothers and children and also prams with false bottoms allowing the base to be filled with a few boilings of peas and the baby put back to sleep over them. Away from the locals at the other end of the field the gypsies would be working together, but a wise man on the weighing machine would tip the hampers of peas before weighing, in case a brick or large stone had accidentally fallen in to the bottom.

The three-horse wagons would pull across the field to the stack of peas and bring them through the village to meet the 4 o'clock train at Bidford siding. This meant that picking was over for the day, but since many had made a six o'clock start, they were glad to make for home. In earlier days many children stayed away from school at pea picking but the new school attendance officer, Bobby Lester, [114] with flowing beard, was hot on the trail of absentees. It was a great shock when he turned up at Bidford Church on Good Friday with his magic lantern with hissing acetylene cylinders for illumination.

Further down Staple Hill in the allotment grounds, gooseberries and currant picking had commenced with just the smallholders' families working together, mostly the women and children, because the men would be picking over the ripest of the *'River's Early Prolific'* or early *'Victoria'* before the great rush with *'Egg' Plums* and *'Belle de Vain'* for the jammers.

The boy coming to school would meet the Co-op bread van, a Model T Ford, making its way to Mickleton and the Cotswold villages, and when Honeybourne lamb sales were on, flocks of several hundred sheep were being driven through the village and up Staple Hill, their shepherds, with attendant faithful sheep dogs, trying to keep ahead of the flock behind and not catch up with the foremost group. The farmers along the route saw to it that all gates were shut, but if there was any sign of straying, the intelligent dogs seemed to have foresight of this happening and were soon turning the leaders who had broken away back on to the highway.

It was only recently that a telephone had been installed at Bickmarsh Hall and saved the unfortunate telegram boy, John Osborne,[115] at Bidford Post Office, finding himself walking up to Bickmarsh and back with market messages from Smithfield at Birmingham, although postcards with orders had overnight delivery and today's post service surely has something to learn from those old postmen on foot and cycle.

Stripped osiers drying by Bidford Bridge *(Permission of Rodney Crompton)*

Some of the boys would fill their school bottles from the house well at China Square. Although only two feet deep, a pure spring gushed ice cold water from the depth of lias stone. This never failed, even in drought.

At the bridge, Gardner's men would be preparing for the busy osier harvest, the early morning sun glinting on the swaying rods with an occasional variety showing blood-red bark which stood out in parcels among the common ochre and bluey Brunswick bunches. The men's sharp *billhook* made short work of each stump sprouting a couple of dozen rods of a year's growth, and as they moved through the *osiernate* there would be a scurry of water vole, sly and silent otter or a clackety dispersal of moorhens or *dabchicks* across the river to the safety of the majestic elms bordering the churchyard and old towpath.

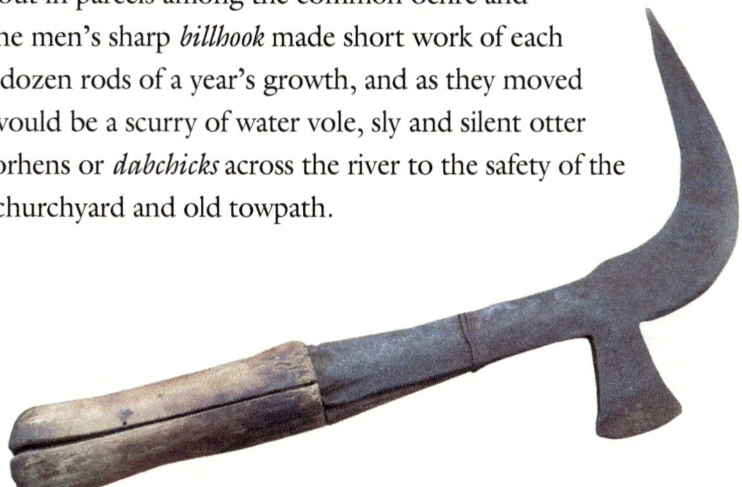

Summer Broom

The Broom boys were always late for school as much was going on, the steam wagons at the Mill getting ready for their journeys or perhaps an unusual train at the junction. All London Underground coaches were brought from Birmingham through Broom and Bidford. They were the same gauge, 4 ft 8½ inches, and were resplendent in red livery and towed by a large 4.6.0 engine which looked quite out of character. Another distraction was when Wilson's Trinity Engines[116] with attendant trailers and Ginny Horse Roundabouts were heard approaching the Green Highway,[117] with spiral stems of polished brass, and brilliant paintwork scroll lined in contrasting colour, their eight foot rubber-tyred driving wheels and front-mounted generators ready to be belt-driven from the spinning fly wheel, all covered with a gaudy wooden roof with sides lettered in gold leaf, together with a smell of burning coal, clean steam, and hot oil on the bearings of the twin pistons which ran at high speed. These road engines were quite different from the slow throb of the machines with winding rope gear used for ploughing and dredging. The road engines too had low geared screw steering. It must have required years of practice for the engineer to spin the wheel, always conscious of the five or six trailer amusement wagons, water cart and sumptuous living caravan with window glass finely decorated with cut and ground and fine plate glass, and always remembering his water pick-up places carefully noted in his travel book.

But to return to these Broom boys, who were experienced scrumpers with an excellent choice of orchards depending on whether they were ready or not. John W Lane's[118] *'Worcester Permain'* orchard was well considered, Slaughter's pear orchard,[119] now built over by the High School, looked over with its juicy *William* pears, but the handy plums of continuing variety in 'Spreading Oak' allotments required careful scrutiny, since one smallholder at work had his eye cocked for any invasion of other small orchards.

These men kept a few pigs in decrepit sties and were not believed when they said that

Winnett's Butcher's High Spring Trap.
(Permission of Rodney Crompton)

pigs could see the wind, and yet, 12 hours before windy squalls, the spiders would be seen busy strengthening their webs and bracing them back secure and tight in the hedgerows. And nearby were mash tubs for soaking grains collected from Stratford Brewery when they were returning empty from market.

The boys would meet the normal road traffic, perhaps Winnett's Butcher's High Spring Trap van with slender wheels and high stepping colt, the butcher's boys clean with snow white smock and apron, having left their blue striped apron in the shop. Winnett's slaughterhouse and shop turned out butchers second to none. Apart from absolute cleanliness, the boys were told as far as food was concerned to 'eat it going along' and get on with it.

The children were also concerned with dandelion and elderberry picking for wine. This was brewed and *barmed* away into the barrels before the great rush to make plum jerkum. It was usual to be on parsnip *(Tanglefoot)* for plum picking, but some preferred rhubarb because this did not give quite so much of a head the next morning. This had been made in the spring when the roots showed a bit of top growth which helped to clear it. Besides it got a bit too potent towards Christmas when it drew clear and clung round the glass. There was no need to write down the recipe for plum jerkum: two pots egg plums, 1 cwt sugar from the Co-op, all in the 30 gallon barrel and top it up with water. Stand ups were best because the top rim could be filled to cover the bung hole and let the ferment gurgle through without air returning to the cask. Nowadays, patent plastic air locks are fussed about with.

AUTUMN

Autumn Cranhill

In the early autumn Cranhill fields, Summer Hill and Caly Cutting were a mecca for blackberry pickers. Families with baskets, buckets and baths made themselves picking hooks to pull down the briars and hump the fruit away in prams and old trucks down to Fred Holder's and his Birmingham market, and if those choosy Brummies could only have seen the receptacles and picking capers, they would have been more than surprised. Some came down Caly allotments and may have seen Caroline Osborne[120] among her straw bee skips, making sure that her swarms in May which were worth a load of hay 'were settling down and working nicely'. The 'swarms of June which were worth a silver spoon' would not be quite so active and anyway the 'swarms of July which were not worth a butterfly' made short shrift in the towering elm crotches.

Some berry pickers liked 'Sinfoil hedges' on Grange Banks, not that the fruit was any blacker, but the adjoining Summer Meadows of Grange Farm were abundant with mushrooms if they could get there early enough, and these made the same journey to Birmingham.

But this was tricky gathering because Gardner's men had cut their osiers just over the river at Barton. The bundles of 100 rods were laid with their *butts* away from the sun ready for floating down to the rod works and it seemed no strange coincidence for Bidford that the large pontoons were never paddled up the river, better to plant the beds upstream and let them float down.

The rod works next to the Pleasure Boat was a brick-floored, below road level building adjoining the Gardners' cottage. The bundles were stacked in the yard,

Pleasure Boat Inn,
BOATS & PUNTS FOR HIRE.
By Hour or Day.
Luncheons & Teas
Large or Small Parties Catered for.
Our English Ham and Egg Teas a Speciality.
LUCAS'S BEST BITTER ALES
WINES and STOUTS.
Supplied by
C. WILSHAW, Proprietress.

those for peeling in a water trough and those for common *pot hampers* near the rear wall. Over all pervaded the stench of barrels of rotten meat for fishing bait in competition with the bitter gall of withy bark. The men laid the bundles at the side of each woman's forked prong ready for her to pull the rod through and reverse it to clear the butt, and the lily white rods would be railed off at Bidford siding to the basket makers.

Longford's would be getting ready for wintertime, the shepherd making sure his split withy hurdles were handy to the fields put down to *mangolds*, to be thrown into heaps and sheeped off in sections. It was a well-known saying interpreted politely that a sheep with the wind was better than a herd of cows and their end labours.

The steam plough engineer would be checking over his outfit, especially the ropes if they had been used on gravel soil or over a banked field, high in the centre, which caused the rope to cut in under tension. The engineers each had their pet *rope-walk* to fit the new lines. These were all of 850 yards long and the new coil would be laid on a drive or flat grassland without twists or curls, one end attached to the front of one engine, having secured the other end of the rope to the second engine winding drum. They would put her quietly in drum gear and slowly lug the free engine back to the second engine, thus ensuring that the drum cable was stowed true and ready for work.

To get steam up the fireman would put in a handful of straw and a few dry hawthorn *'kettle hangers'* out of the bottom of the hedge. Now straw gives off a pungent thick smoke and if this started pouring from the fire lid and ash grating, he knew at once that, whilst the engine had been standing idle under the hedge, some mischievous boy had lifted the smoke stack lid and popped in a wad of sack bags. However, the more sophisticated pranksters would chuck in a couple of handfuls of salt into the tubes. This was just as effective, and even stopped fire lighting operations after the old engineer had checked the stack.

Opposite: An advert for the Pleasure Boat Inn in the Bidford Improvements Association Horse Races and Sports Carnival Official Programme,
Thursday 9th August 1928. Bidford Improvements Association, 1928

Autumn Bickmarsh and Barton

The large rolling fields of Bickmarsh Farm were heavy headed with wheat, although some were put down to oats and barley for stock feeding and the Hall had a mill with grinding stones and these were recut and set up in the 1939-45 war.

The boys were useful at harvest for bond tying after the reapers who had cut a way round close to the hedge, giving a space for the horses pulling the binder to walk without waste or damage to the crop.

The men with hand sickle, or rather *bagging hook*, made left-handed or right-handed depending on the *crock* near the handle, and a nut or ash *fagging hook* cut from the hedge would take about six rows of wheat about six feet long. Holding the fagging hook at the top to let it fall one way, they would cut to the end of the *drift* and then back with both hooks and, with help from their knees, make the sheaf and lie it flat for the following boy. He, taking a few straws, would slip it round and finish with a quick half turn knot.

Now the binder would arrive, having travelled cross-wise to its normal direction since the travelling wheels were removed, and the machine set down on its wide driving wheel. The *sails* would be erected, the side six foot segmented blade slid in place and the canvasses which lifted up the cut wheat to the bonder and knotter adjusted. This knotter was a remarkable piece of equipment. It was threaded up with binder twine from 9 lb balls, two being carried in a round string box and the balls knotted together for continuous running. As the straw filled the receiving arms, the large needle would sweep the twine round the bundle and then this clever knot automatically tied the string, cut the bond and the sheaf thrown out.

Two horses and *pole gearing* were the usual motive power but on *siding* and hilly fields an extra horse making three abreast or perhaps a foremost couple were used. All being set, the driver would climb up on to the high seat at the rear, thread his *G.O. Lines* through a *stay* to keep them clear of the flying *sails* and set off with a clatter of gears and shuttling canvas.

Now came another boy's job, *stooking*. After his sheafs had been grabbed by the head, they were stood against each other, then against four others to complete the stook and finally stood firm to ripen the corn and fine weather prayed for. Oats by tradition 'saw three Sundays' in the field. The stooks also were good cover for rabbits because as the binder got nearer the centre, they began to bolt, but they were wise to the fact that if a small part of the field was left uncut overnight they had better make their departure.

It was soon carrying time. The wagons already used for *haysel* would turn into the field with a boy riding the *foremost*. On the wagon was the loader with short-handled *shuppick* and after filling the bottom he would start courses all round with the *butts* outwards. The pitchers either side set the pace but if they set too mad a pace, it was easy to kick off a sheaf or two and they did not like second throwing when the load was high.

A properly made load would carry to the corner rick position. The wagons were drawn close either side and the *trace horses* shut off and taken by the boy to help in the next loaded wagon. It was the ricker's job to bring the walls up slightly, although in a round rick it was a continuous spiral course, pushing out each sheaf and filling in to the centre with set courses. This was an interesting example of fellowship among men because they themselves may be the person to cast off at threshing time and, if not, their mates knew how the sheaves lay for clearing.

At eaves level a *pitching hole* was left for a man to stand for the second lift to form the roof. Of course this is where the ricker had his own back. It was easy to bowl them down from the wagon when the rick was young, but a different proposition as the rick grew. It was necessary for the pitch hole man to stab the flying sheaf with his fork and to catch the momentum of the rising sheaf making it easier to get it up to the ricker.

The ridge of the rick was finished off with a single flat course of sheaves laid end to end. This allowed the rick to sweat and a well-made rick should shed off any but the heaviest rain from the ends of the slanting *butts.*

A great pride was taken in making a firm upright rick because any lack of skill in coursing showed when the rick settled down. A leaning wall was difficult to correct for thatching. If any doubt existed, the rick was propped on the leaning side hoping that the high side would correct this on settlement, but it was an unforgiveable sin for this excuse of bad workmanship and every passer-by saw the red-faced shame of the man concerned.

After all was safely gathered in and the last sheaf carried down from the field, a week or two would elapse before the thatcher came with his bundle of traps, and specially long ladder able to lie on the roof from apex to the ground. He would have his bundles of split withy rick pegs about 2 feet long, and push in about six or eight of them spaced out down the right hand side of the ladder from top to bottom. These were *left proud* about five inches and his coils of binder twine tied on, a neat layer of straw laid overlapping from bottom to top. The ladder was now moved over about a foot to the left, sometime humping the top over before he came down to move the foot.

The second line of pegs was then arranged and the coils of twine brought across the lay of straw. All except the first row of pegs were now pushed home in turn to tighten the thatch. After continuing this process round the rick, the twine was fixed to the first struck pegs, which were pushed home and the job completed.

The thatcher with his wooden rake would work round the rick area and leave it neat and tidy, yet another example of good workmanship because there was bound to be a bit of weed growth before threshing. Besides, who would want to traipse through rotting straw when the engine and threshing box would soon lay down any split corn which had *chitted* and begun to grow in the cycle of nature without man's help.

Meanwhile it was time for the steam *scuffling* of the stubble. If this was done soon after carrying and a lucky break of autumn sun prevailed, many weeds were killed and the ground was in better condition for the plough. During the summer months George Moore,[121] the Bickmarsh blacksmith, had been servicing the engines and gear for autumn work.

This was a dirty and dusty job and many a boy's holiday was spent riding the scuffle to return home simply grimy. If he was helpful to the engineer, however, it was his heyday of delight to be allowed to move up the engine, but soon powerful arms were requested to straighten up the chain and rack steering and wide-rimmed forward wheels.

The outfit consisted of two engines, living van, with large stowage lockers between the chassis members, water cart and a couple of heavy trailers for implements and coal bunkers. The first engine would set in at the far end of the field towing the scuffle and attached to the rope of the gear-free second engine ready for the first *bout* back across the field. The scuffle was left facing the second engine. Number one would put his winding drum out of cog and give a toot on his whistle. This was the signal for Number 2 to let in the long lateral arm to the forward steam cocks, the pistons would begin to receive, the huge fly-wheel gathered momentum, and the drum gear was quietly engaged for a steady start to take up the slack rope to prevent snatching and a broken cable. As soon as all was taut and strained Number 2 would pick up immense power. The gradual increase of piston speed as more steam forced the stroke was sometimes accompanied by a rising burst of black smoke from the chimney stack as the engineer underblew his fire from his steam jet to make it draw and keep plenty of pressure in hand.

When the scuffle had nearly finished its journey across the field, the operator would drop in the lifting sprocket for the wheels to lift the legs. The engine man moved forward, the width of the scuffle pulling the implement half way round, and then disengaged his drum. Then it was time for his whistle signal and Number 1, having moved up also sometime previously when running slack to save a few moments when they were on piecework, now set his drum in to give the scuffle its last half turn and work across another bout. The field having been completed, the drum would be towed tight to each returning engine to lift up the soil and loosen the wheel track marks. Another whistle signal, however, was very necessary. If the scuffle on its rolling gait across the field became fast, progress was halted until Number 2 engineer with a free gear sounded two hoots on the whistle and engaged his drum to lug back the implement.

Rope splicing was interesting to watch. The Warwickshire bred John Allen[122] had retired to his cottage near the blacksmith's shop. His successor, Arthur Whiting,[123] a Gloucester man, also retired, lived nearby. Blackwells brought down a broken rope to be welded, a sign of changing times, and the two old engineers had a fine time of argument between

Allen's right-handed Warwickshire splice and Whiting's Gloucester left-handed method. This must have made their day until the blacksmith wheeled out his bottle of oxygen and acetylene indicating that old arts and crafts had been laid aside with modern methods.

The beauty of rope work was that no engine weight padded the centre land as tractor wheels do moving up and down. An attempt was made to use diesel engines for rope working, but they did not stand up to the steady powerful steam engines which, when going was hard, simply steadied themselves until pressure release, which combustion engines were not able to do.

The engine crew on piecework made a very early start and sometimes slept in the van because the fire had to be raked out about 3 am after overnight banking to raise steam and the attendant horse-drawn water cart man was soon called on. These tanks, hand pumped full from the nearest pond, had *baffle plates* fitted inside because the water-sway sometimes moved the *filler* horse and was most necessary to run along the hollows of a

Scratting Box (Permission of Avoncroft Museum)

landed field. Crossing the crests with a heavy load could bring dire results, although an open topped tank could be pressed into service if a couple or three *pot hampers* were floated in it to arrest the sway of water.

Late autumn having arrived, the first frost crept in. Blackberrying finished, none were picked after a frost because this makes them bitter as gall and the birds moved in for their feasting. Apples, however, were being gathered from the floor of the cider orchard. These having been bagged up were taken down to Barton Mill and tipped a few at a time in the circular shallow stone trough. An old horse walking round and never getting anywhere would now be hitched to the strong cross beam attached to the centre stay with a huge mill stone set between. As this was slowly rolled round the trough, the fruit was crushed and the juice run off to waiting hogshead barrels. This operation even crushed the pips and made cider nutty as compared with the *scratting box* method at Welford Water Mill.

The mush was shovelled out periodically into the waiting press and poured into a bottomless box which held the cloth lining firm until the top could be folded over and the box raised for another layer. The press had two large screws and the men who forced these down with crowbars no doubt made good use of the special barrel or two stored since the last year for this purpose. These were always filled with juice that had slowly trickled from the overnight pressing, because this was potent with goodness and body.

An old donkey driven press used in the cider making process.
(Photographer: Andy J Billington. Shutterstock 1438706771)

Broom in Autumn

Broom boys coming to school would meet many loads of wheat coming to the Mills. The three-horse wagons were not really suitable in shape for this job. They held three sacks wide and eight sacks long stood upright, weighing 280 lbs each, and due to the uneven road the wheel hubs could be heard knocking against the side bracket. Although only a small amount of play was allowed when they were made, the wheelwright was wise to this great stress and figured out the spoke camber so that when the spokes were at the bottom of the wheel they were almost upright to carry the load. Wagons had no brakes and at an incline it was necessary to stop and slip on a couple of *skid pans.* Another useful gadget when ascending hills was a small roller trailed close behind the rear wheels which *scotched* the wheel if they were halted.

The wagoner usually walked at the *filler's* head and had *G.O.Lines* to the two *foremost* because wagons had a short lock and could be pitched over with too sharp a turn. Adkins' had no weighbridge at this time, and the one at Broom Junction was busy, all loads going over the bridge for weighing before pulling into the mill. With long wagons on the short weighbridge the load was weighed twice, front wheels on the centre of the large plate and then rear wheels with the front on the hard ground. How the porter worked out his ticket by this fulcrum arrangement I never knew but the load was soon away to the water powered hoist. A chain was attached to the neck, a tug on a clutch chain and the sack disappeared up through three floors lifting back flap floor sections as it went through ready for its slow journey up and down through shuts, elevator buckets for cleaning and sieving, or along to the flour rolling machines. Some horses did not take too kindly to the rushing water of the mill *race* as it left the great paddle wheel and the general hubbub of wheat series and humming machinery with flapping belts.

Broom Mill *(Warwickshire County Record Office PH21/59)*

Broom in Autumn

Some wagoners made a return load with barley meal, *sharps* and *middlings* ground for winter feed and lucky ones were able to scrounge a decent eel from the traps at the overflow of the pound at the rear upstream. Others had spread a *bolting* or two of straw under the load to drop off at some smallholder's with a reward of a jug of home-made.

Other traffic was also on the road, staunch Methodist, Charlie Harris,[124] with his high-covered two-wheeled spring cart delivering oil and candles all around the villages, or loads of *cordwood* from 'Cold Comfort', 'Rosehill'[125] and 'Weethley' Woods for weighing. The faggots for kindling were ready wired in *scores* and some farms had *shoddy* for manure delivered loose in open rail trucks. If there was ever a need for 'dirty-work extra', this was it.

One of the watchers would be Jack Tarver,[126] the length man, keeping the grass verges cut and edging with a single blade *mattock* and making himself completely at ease at lunchtime by tipping his barrow on to the handles with airborne wheel and completely filling the barrow body with his own.

It is probable that an odd one or two of the many thatched cottages needed attention of the Creswells.[127] The fact that their long slender ladders footed themselves into the centre of the road so as to lay flat on the roof never hindered horse traffic. They just drove round and skirted the tidy stacks of drawn straw ready to be laid.

But the boys' favourite hunting ground was under the ancient walnut trees along the *fordraft*. If the saying 'like women and walnut trees' were true, these old limbs had more than their share for between boys' sticks being thrown up and the crafty and cunning rook visitations, they had many wounds. The rooks always built their tree top nests with walnut twigs but they knew when a tree was unsafe and would not be secure till after nesting time. These

A mattock

nests were hammered in rook shoots when parties of men with double-barrelled guns would wait until the fledgling could sit on the side of the nest and then blast off, with an untidy slaughter surrounding the base of the tree while the parents were flying round in mad and wild confusion.

But winter was not far away and the potato picking gangs were busy with their buckets. The long narrow trench was being dug close to the hedge for the carts to tip in their loads of spuds. It was covered with a two-foot layer of hedge croppings and straw followed with a neat padding of coil for frost protection, to await its end opening with hand-turned *rocking riddle* rolling out the large tubers and making a heap of small *pig chats* underneath.

WINTER

Winter Cranhill

The Cranhill boy on his way to school would come out to a fairy wonderland with the intricate fronds of dainty hoar frost on the hedgerows. Most trees had lost their leaves but some of the apple trees were majestic with rosy apples on the bare branches.

The hedges were festooned with *old man's beard* and gaudy with hips and haws in their vermilion glory, some saying it was a sign of a hard winter, and God had provided the birds with food, but this fallacy was only the result of a kind spring and good germinating weather at blossom time. The puddly roads made smashing slides for hob-nailed boots, but a gingerly step on the ponds and boundary brook was required before taking the risk of a long slide or chilling plunge through the cracking ice.

The carrier's horses had paid an early visit to the smith's for frost nailing, while over the hedge the plough teams were making good progress if the frost was not too severe. Wet weather was the ploughman's nightmare. He only had a limited season and in very wet periods the carpenters would fit an ash wooden *shell-board* to keep the slick furrows turning over.

It was the time for nightly prowling with bat fowling nets, watching for where an odd pheasant went to roost, checking over the long rabbit nets and bolting the holes with slipped in ferrets with the resultant merciless squeal as they reached the bottom burrows. Time also on a quiet night for the blood curdling howl of the vixen and the banshee flight of the great ghostly barn owl.

This was the time for heavy winter clothes, corduroy and tweed and homespun cloth purchased with the pea-picking money, the men sporting balaclava helmets and hand-knitted mittens. There was much chuffing and blowing as the engines tried to move off from Bidford siding having only racing driving wheels on the icy track through the cutting. The boy would return home with a brilliant jewel-like sun setting over Evesham in the clear frosty air which stung the nostrils and froze the toes in hard leather boots. Some comfort was obtained by running a heavy iron hoop to school but the out of breath arrival at school, which was cold to sit in with sweaty clothing, made attention to the teacher difficult until everyone was turned out for physical jerks, a round or two of 'Johnny on the Mop Stick'[128] and a session of leap frog. The red-faced and healthy-looking school child of today is vastly different from some of the wizened faced hungry children in handed-down clothes of those days when a cure for whooping cough[129] was to stand near the tar boiler and inhale its noxious fumes. On a rare occasion the huntsmen could be seen in full cry over the distant hills from Cranhill's high vantage point and the foot followers were quick to seize any opportunity to fill the stock pot simmering on the kitchen hob at home, where they often were before even *'Gone Away'* was blown by the huntsman's horn.

Winter Bickmarsh

Hedging and ditching operations skirted the roadside now. First the hedge bottoms were cut out and trimmed leaving the slender saplings tall and bare, swaying in the wind until the hedger returned to the start again to give them a half cut with razor sharp *billock*, and pull them down for weaving in and out of the strong stakes he had picked out, topping with long nut *heatherings* or briar pressed in with his thick leather gloves. It was vital to keep the clay soil ditches running sweet and clean, but it was before the days of wellingtons and some men sowed the seeds of rheumatics in later life by working wet-footed all day with bags tied round their legs to keep some of their trouser legs dry. Some farmers kept a pair of heavy leather jackboots for this job but, although kept well dubbined, a weakening stitch soon proved its unworthiness with leaking, squelching sole. The proud worker left a work of art with trimmed stakes and hedge bottom and ditch side plastered with slick clay sods by spade or *ditching grout.*

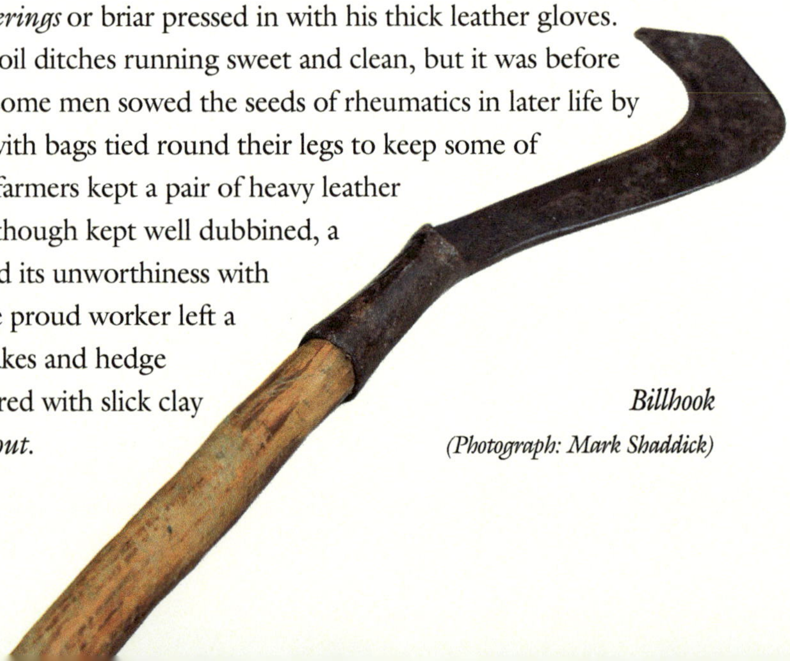

Billhook
(Photograph: Mark Shaddick)

Bickmarsh Hall *(Warwickshire County Record Office EAC402)*

The *store cattle's* high racks were kept filled with the rougher hay and straw and the sheep trough, with close wire frames and iron circular roofs topped up, set among the hurdled flocks between turnips and *mangold*, the sweetest hay being kept for the milking cows to ensure the milk returns were kept up and save on dear imported cattle cake.

Near the Bridge the lonely *'Molly Hearns'* were *tracing* the river, irate for now scarce food and perhaps the Avon was edged with creeping ice away from the faster flowing centre. This was always tested, sometimes with dire results when the sinking floes began to crack, by the boys who were marched down to football on Friday afternoon. Sometimes swans wandered into High Street with shy gait for food scraps, having mercilessly driven away their changing colour cygnets to their own devices and feeding grounds at Grange.

The boys returning home in the gathering dusk were sometimes surprised by an early marauding owl which gave rise to many ghost stories. The Hall at Bickmarsh had its ghost, of sorts. An occupant owed much money and since his debts died with him, all was well until a couple of poachers flushing out a wood pile saw him walking in the moonlight in the grounds six months after the funeral. Since there was no escape for either party, the truth revealed that the coffin buried in Bidford churchyard had contained a flitch of bacon and the day of reckoning had arrived.

Father was now having a busy evening or two sawing up *cordwood* in the hovel usually found in the rear garden, and some of the men would mate together with long twin-handled cross cut saws, wide set and helped through with a mug of cider and a nick of *twist* in their clay pipes.

Winter Broom

'Old Stanley',[130] the local undertaker at Broom, would note that 'a green Christmas meant a full churchyard', but death was also around in the visit of the pig killer, having ascertained which day he would be able to attend, and more important at what time because towards Christmas he might kill eight or ten bacon pigs in a day's work. The sties were small and a 16 or 20 *score* pig did not have much room to move which required crafty shunting about without upsetting the animal and getting it excited. Father would not feed her from the previous evening and by morning light, hungry grunts and squeals were abroad.

Mother, having specially scrubbed out the copper in the washhouse, would be up to light an early fire because lots of hot water was required. Meanwhile, father had placed his pig bench (about 4 feet x 18 inches x one and half inch elm top on four strong splayed feet) near to the sty and laid handy a couple of *boltings* of wheat straw. The butcher, having put on his blue killing apron and strapped on his square leather knife pouch, would roll up his bloody coil of twine and gander over to the sty. By this time the pig had gathered something was afoot. The butcher now set his noose, almost like a lasso, slipped it round the pig's jaws so that the more the pig pulled, the tighter it became. The pig usually backed away into a corner and this was the signal for about three stalwart helpers to enter, one to the tail, and one each side. The pig was now cajoled, pushed, pulled and shoved along the side of the bench and deftly rolled over by the butcher on to the top and his bottom legs quickly roped under the bench. The helpers now lay across the pig, watching out for flaying legs. The butcher would now lift a front leg and quickly slip his sticking

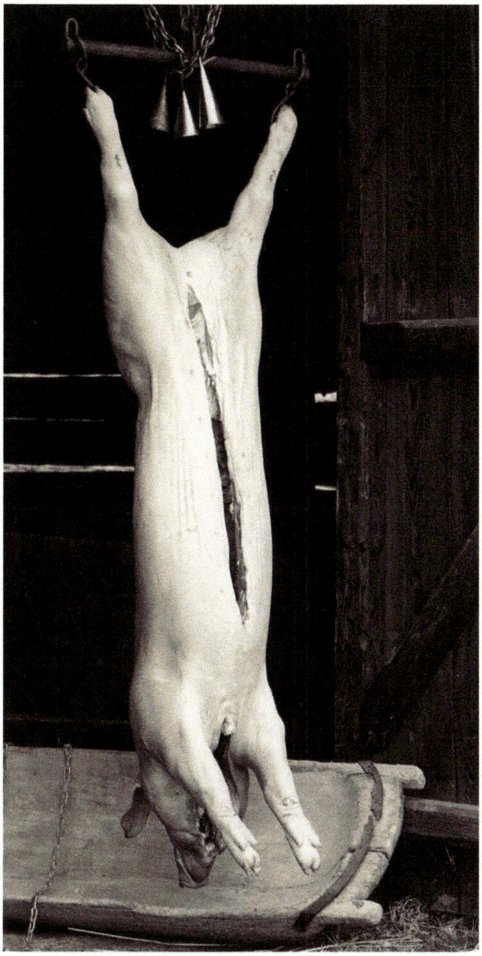

knife into the jugular vein. The first spurts of blood proved his skill, and he would start pumping the leg for complete bleeding. This actually took less time to do than write about it.

Everybody now took a breather and the pig lay straddled on the bench, care being taken not to bruise it as the salt would not otherwise take effect when curing. The pig was now laid upright, fore and hind legs stretched on straw and tightly covered with more straw. This was fired from the rear end and gently moved with the butcher's *shuppick* to completely burn off all hair without heat cracking the rind. This completed, the pig was lain on his back on clean straw and his feet horns snatched off with a hook iron. He was now ready for disembowelling with a long shallow cut from neck to groin. First out was the complete pluck, i.e. liver, heart and *lights*. These were placed on a dish for faggot making. Then the *leaf for lard* spread on a cross stick like a coat hanger and hung in the nearest tree to set. After this, the kell or stomach lining for covering faggots. A bath was now placed ready to receive the belly for *chitterlings* after turning and salting for several days.

The pig was now carried by the helpers to the brewhouse where a permanent strong iron hook was fixed to the roof and the carcase was lifted until the hook could catch in the roof of the mouth and then everything nicely washed down and bets laid as to how many *score* it was. Next day, the carcase being stiff, it was lowered on to the bench and cut into hams, flitches and the heads into *chawls*, the fillet pieces removed for someone's lucky breakfast. All was now ready for salting. The pieces were laid in block salt on the stone trough with shallow sides to contain the brine, and salt petre rubbed into the ham joints for deep penetration, and sometimes brown sugar for flavour. After about a month in pickle the pieces dried and were put in muslin linen and hung on the wall or rested on the usual kitchen bacon rack on the ceiling. Indeed, most cottages had a 'picture on the wall' in the shape of a ham of 40 to 50 lbs.

The helpers had a share of the cut meat and, when their killing came, theirs would be shared out also. Indeed, it was 'living like lords' for a time, and taste of real home-cured bacon has never been supplanted by any modern methods.

Another source of Christmas cash where children could help was poultry plucking and a few of the Broom flock were experts. Cockerel picking was pretty straightforward. They had more than likely been killed by sticking a sharp pointed knife into the roof of the mouth and then hung up to flap and expire flicking blood all around. One dodge was to hold the feet and dip the carcase quickly into boiling water, but if they could press on soon after killing while the blood was warm, the operation was much easier. Turkeys were usually rough-plucked for market and long hanging in the shop, but the cottagers really earned their money with geese. To start with, it was quite a strenuous caper to kill them with their great strength and sense of survival, and a back kitchen was set aside for picking. The workers sat on *pot hampers* or old armchairs with open fire place. As work became more hectic, most of the floor was covered with feathers and geese even made their hair flutter with fairy-like floating specks of down. At the rear of the cottage or up the garden was a burning place with a continuing fire flaring up when a tidy-up was imperative and the resultant smell of oily quill, topped by the entrails after drawing had finished, pervaded the whole neighbourhood. Fridges and cold-rooms were to be of the affluent future as all the work was carried out in the twelve days before Christmas, although some butchers and fishmongers like the Nailors[131] under the Assembly Rooms, had a delivery of huge 56 lbs blocks of ice from Evesham to help storage problems.

The old scissor and knife sharpener would have his eye to business and make one of his calls near Christmas. Between villages he would push his two-wheeled truck, but this was quickly converted for use by turning it half over which made a seat of the towing handles and there he would sit treadling away the grindstone with nearby tray of *carborundum* and whet stones for finishing off. One traveller who had an inventive nature fitted his gear to a push cycle which worked by manipulation of chain and belt when it was stood on the carrier stand. It gave quicker movement between villages. The grinder would collect the cutlery from a whole street and set up at the corner to show he was about and available and everyone trusted him to return the knives and scissors knowing that he would be around again, sooner or later, when pea-picking, plum-picking and other kindred jobs had been completed.

An advert for Stanley Nailor in the Bidford Improvements Association Horse Races and Sports Carnival Official Programme, Thursday 9th August 1928. Bidford Improvements Association, 1928

Endnotes

1. The Education Act of 1891 made elementary education free for all children. Prior to this date, most children paid a penny a week in fees, although many poor children were exempted.
2. The office of 'Overseer' dates back to the Elizabethan Poor Law of 1597, as a result of which overseers were responsible for attending to the welfare of the poor at parish level. This involved the setting and administering of the poor rate and providing 'indoor relief' in the workhouse and various forms of 'outdoor relief'. It may be viewed as an early experiment in care in the community. Under the Poor Law Amendment Act of 1834 Overseers were replaced by Boards of Guardians, but even after the local Government Act of 1894 transferred many of the functions of the Boards to the newly created Parish Councils, the office of Overseer continued to be an important element in parochial administration, especially in rural parishes, until it was abolished in 1927.
3. Following the setting up of the National Society in 1811 to provide elementary education for the poor in accordance with 'the principles of the Established Church', a small National School was built in Church Street and enlarged in the 1840s to accommodate 160 children. When a new National School was erected in Victoria Road in 1872, 'the Old School' continued to be used as an Infant Department until 1950 after which time the building became the Church Hall.
4. 'Lizzie' Smith lived in Marlcliff and rode to school on a bicycle. She was sister to William Smith of Clay Hall Farm. One of her pupils, Mollie Henderson, described her as 'kind and patient', and on her retirement in 1932 the Vicar, Rev Albert Harrison, wrote of the 'great esteem and respect' in which she was held.
5. Miss Quail started as an Assistant Teacher at the Infants School in October 1914 when the Head Teacher was Miss Minnie Moore. Sometime between 1918 and 1921 she succeeded Miss Moore as Head and continued in the post until at least 1925. She was described by one of her pupils as 'a very austere lady' who was not

afraid to use the cane. During her time at the school she lived in a cottage on Tower Hill.

6. Albert Warner was Headmaster of Bidford Junior School from July 1917 to July 1946. He was noted for his strict discipline and certainly did not 'spare the rod'.
7. Mr Warner believed strongly in the importance of music in the school curriculum and introduced lessons in musical appreciation. Some of these were surprisingly highbrow. In the School Log for 12th March 1926, he wrote: 'I have taken the story of Wagner's *Parsifal* with the top classes this week...and at 3 o'clock the Rev Sheard... brought some HMV records of the opera which were played to the children'.
8. *Zurika the Gypsy Maid* was an operetta for children, alternatively known as *The Captive Princess.* It was composed in 1904 by Clementine Ward who wrote numerous operettas for children during the first decade of the 20th century.
9. First performed in 1871, *The Merrie Men of Sherwood Forest* was a pastoral operetta in three acts, written and composed by W H Birch (1826–88).
10. Samuel George Mason (1862-1938) lived at Bowood House on Salford Road, and is listed in the Trade Directories for 1924 – 1932 as a fruit farmer. He took a keen interest in ancient monuments and played a leading role in the restoration of Bidford Bridge. In 1920 he was one of the founder members of the Dugdale Society, named after the eminent Warwickshire antiquary, Sir William Dugdale (1605-1686). The Society was set up with the aim of preserving and publishing original documents relating to the history of the county. Now over a century old, the Society continues to fulfil this aim to the benefit of local historians in particular.
11. Rev Arthur Edward William Sheard was Rector of Exhall from 1905 to 1940. For much of this period he was Diocesan Inspector for Religious Instruction.
12. Song of the Flea was a popular song composed by the Russian composer Modest Mussorgsky (1839-81) and still a concert favourite today. Mussorgsky wrote four operas, the most famous being *Boris Godunov*.
13. 'Caly' is a shortened form of 'California', a loosely defined locality less than a mile eastwards from the centre of Bidford. When and why the term first came to be used remains obscure. 'California Cottage' was an isolated dwelling on the Stratford Road during the 1920s. Nowadays, the Health Centre and other houses are situated close by.
14. The station was built as an exchange platform on the so-called Gloucester Loop

Line from Barnt Green to Ashchurch when the Stratford-upon-Avon and Midland Junction Railway opened in 1879. The loop line was built in four stages between 1859 and 1868. It connected stations along its route including Redditch, Alcester and Evesham, Broom and Salford Priors with the main line from Birmingham to Gloucester. Providing easy access for passengers and freight traffic, Broom Junction proved much more popular than Bidford's own station.

15. Bidford and Binton stations, both opened in 1885, were the only two stations on the Stratford-upon-Avon and Midland line between Broom Junction and Stratford. Bidford station consisted of a single-route platform with a siding and goods yard next to Bidford Brick Works. By 1922 the goods yard incorporated a coal yard. The station offered a limited passenger service, only four trains per day in each direction for much of the period from 1905 to 1938. Passenger services were terminated in 1947. More important for the village was the transportation of goods in and out of the station, especially the marketing of locally produced fruit and vegetables. Such freight traffic continued until 1960.
16. The spot from which Jack Moore claims the eight churches could be seen has yet to be identified. Changes in the landscape during the intervening period have made it unverifiable.
17. Primrose Castle, more commonly known as Oversley Castle, was originally built as an eye catcher on the site of an old British fort at the suggestion of the Prince Regent, later George IV, on one of his many visits to the 2nd Marquis of Hertford at Ragley Hall. The 'castle' has recently been demolished. Primrose Hill is situated a little to the north, overlooking the main A46, Evesham to Stratford Road.
18. According to an 18th century legend, Shakespeare's Crab refers to the crab-apple tree under which, or in which, William Shakespeare is alleged to have spent the night recovering from a hangover after he and some Stratford friends were involved in a drinking contest with the Bidford Sippers at the Falcon Inn. When asked the following morning if he wished to resume drinking, Shakespeare is said to have declared:

    'I have drunk with
    Piping Pebworth, Dancing Marston
    Haunted Hillborough, Hungry Grafton
    Dodging Exhall, Papist Wixford
    Beggarly Broom and Drunken Bidford
    And I can drink no more'.

19. He was probably the Jesse Houghton who was born in Knowle, Worcestershire in 1878, one of the ten children of Thomas and Ellen Houghton. By 1881 the family was living in Icknield Street. His father was a stonemason and by 1901 Jesse was employed as a bricklayer. He married Julia Emily Wilcox, by whom he had three children. After joining the armed forces in 1916, and serving in the army of occupation in Germany after the war, he returned to Bidford to resume his employment as a bricklayer. He died in 1930.
20. 'Sinfoil bank' is not marked on any maps of the period. 'Sinfoil' may be a local corruption of the plant name 'Cinquefoil', a common name for 'Potentilla reptans', whose bright yellow flowers and five-lobed leaves flourish on dry, grassy banks. However, historically, the fodder crop, 'sainfoin' ('healthy hay') was also commonly known as 'Cinquefoil'. This vetch-like plant, with plumed pink flowers is in the pea family. Its botanical name, 'Onobrychis viciifolia', means 'greedily devoured by donkeys'!
21. Born Muriel Pringle in 1885, she married Henry Marston Layard Crawford in 1908, following which her husband took up a post as assistant to the ageing Dr Hobbes in Bidford. In 1912 they moved from The Harbour after purchasing in her name Avonside House in Grange Road and had it converted into 'a fine example of the arts and crafts building tradition'. Under the pseudonym 'Muriel Marston', she wrote three illustrated books describing different aspects of the gardens she had created: *A Garden by the Avon* (1933), *Garden Magic* (1934) and *Who Loves a Garden* (1936). In 1939 the Crawfords went to live at The Cockpit, subsequently Blythe House, which they had built for them in the grounds of Avonside.
22. Born in Evesham in 1879, John Cole lived to the ripe old age of 91. In 1911 he was living in Salford Road with wife and young family and employed as a foreman market gardener. His later position with the Crawfords at Avonside is confirmed by the entry in the 1939 Register where his employment is recorded as 'chauffeur-gardener'.
23. This is a likely reference to Edwin Sheasby, born in 1886 in Stoke near Coventry. He was the son of Arthur Sheasby, a bricklayer and his wife Harriet, a native of Bidford. Shortly after his birth, the family moved to Bidford and lived in Icknield Street. In 1902 Edwin enlisted as a regular soldier with the Royal Garrison Artillery, returning to Bidford by 1911 to work alongside his father. During the period leading up to the outbreak of war he assisted Mrs Crawford in designing the Avonside garden. Tragically, Edwin died in March 1915 on active service in France,

after contracting pneumonia.

24. Avonside was one of numerous emergency maternity homes set up as part of government policy to protect the unborn generation. From 1940 to 1945 hundreds of expectant mothers, particularly from Birmingham and Coventry, came to Avonside to have their babies in the relative security of the Warwickshire countryside. The hospital was also made available to local women experiencing difficult pregnancies and acted as a recovery centre for wounded airmen from the nearby air bases at Honeybourne and Long Marston.
25. Blue Lias stone was formed between 195 and 200 million years ago. The stone is a visible feature of the cliffs on the Jurassic coast in Dorset, especially around Lyme Regis and Charmouth, where the rock is rich in fossils. Many variations of blue lias are to be found across the country. Warwickshire has numerous outcrops, its distinctive variety being known as Wilmcote Limestone which is blue-grey in colour and makes excellent building stone. It was quarried at several locations to the north and west of Stratford, particularly at Wilmcote, Binton and Grafton, although these quarries had been largely worked out by the early 20th century and few traces now remain. Several buildings in Bidford bear evidence of blue lias, including the bridge, the Parish Church and the old Falcon Inn. It was also used in the building of nearby Ragley Hall at the end of the 17th century and, most prestigiously, in the flooring of parts of the new Houses of Parliament following the disastrous fire of 1834.
26. Henry Marston Layard Crawford (1881-1943) came to Bidford in 1906 as assistant doctor to the ageing Dr Hobbes. He had a distinguished record as a Medical Officer during the First World War and was awarded the Military Cross in 1918. After Dr Hobbes' retirement, he became the senior partner in the practice. Dr Crawford's health deteriorated during the last years of his life and in the months leading up to his death he became blind. As a mark of affection and respect for his work in the village, the Crawford Memorial Hall was erected in 1955. See also Endnote 21.
27. George Burdett (1837-1921) is listed in the 1881 and 1891 Censuses as a Carrier, and in 1901 as a Carrier and Coal Merchant. His address in each is recorded as Town's End (now Grange Road). The wharf itself was accessed from the High Street and situated near the Roman causeway.
28. Probably a reference to the Thomas Taylor who was born in Bidford in 1864. His father, Richard, was an agricultural labourer and his mother, Hannah, worked as a

glove maker, a trade which provided numerous Bidford women with domestic employment during the 19th and early 20th centuries. For at least 20 years Thomas' occupation was that of 'general labourer', but by 1911 he was employed as a carter for a local coal merchant, and lived in the High Street with his wife, Annie, and their three daughters, the eldest of whom, Lucy, was engaged in agricultural work. Thomas died in 1939.

29. As a young man in his twenties, Jack Percival Styles (1912-1973), then living and working in Stratford-upon-Avon, was appointed choirmaster at St Laurence's Parish Church and also conducted the WI Choir. During the 1930s the Boys Choir won six successive first prizes at the Leamington Music Festival. After serving in the armed forces during the Second World War, he continued as Choirmaster until 1947, when he was appointed Organist and Choirmaster at Hampton Lucy. His wife, Kitty, was a noted writer of children's books featuring the adventures of the cat, Nicholas Thomas.
30. In 1910 Harry and Edmund Crane founded the Hercules Cycle & Motor Co Ltd. The Company started in the back streets of Balsall Heath before moving to the former Dunlop factory in Aston in 1923. By 1927 the 'Britannia Works', as it became known, was producing 250,000 cycles per year. The Hercules Lion is the mascot of Aston Villa Football Club.
31. William Hawes Longford's occupancy of Tower Hill Farm extended from the early years of the century until his death in 1940. It was one of the largest farms in the Bidford area during the inter-war period, its fields stretching down to the River Avon. His middle daughter, Dorothy, did not marry and for several years organised the gymkhana for the annual Bidford Carnival. She cut a striking figure riding side saddle, dressed in a long skirt and wearing a top hat.
32. Tangye and Bros was a Birmingham engineering company which produced the first British gas engine in 1881. After World War I, the company began the production of industrial diesel engines, but, after the Second World War, stopped engine production and concentrated on making hydraulic pumps and valves. In 1869 they were commissioned to design the hydraulic systems for the first funicular cliff railway in Scarborough and were also responsible for the design of the Saltburn Cliff Lift, which today is the oldest water-powered cliff railway in Britain.
33. George Henry (Harry) Odell (1865-1939) ran a flourishing milk business which by 1936 had been taken over by his son-in-law, George Cope.

34. During the 1850s Edwin Foden of Sandbach began designing and manufacturing a range of agricultural and industrial machines including steam engines, and in 1901 produced his first steam driven wagon. His competitively priced wagons were known for their simplicity and elegance of design and became especially popular with brewers and light hauliers.
35. The Sentinel truck was originally a steam-powered road vehicle for carrying freight. In 1906 Alley and McLellan launched the first Sentinel wagon, the earliest form of lorry, which was superseded in the 1930s by motorised vehicles.
36. Gilbert Arthur Boshier (1882-1955) was born in Farnborough, near Banbury. His father, William, was a Farm and Estate Steward for the Holbeche Estate. By 1908, after working as a steam engine maker, Gilbert had moved to Bidford and set up in business as a garage proprietor in the High Street, the single petrol pump outside his house becoming a feature of the village landscape for many years. In the early 1920s he was joined by his architect brother, George. George's wife, Ethel, was a trained nurse and acted as the village midwife for much of the inter-war period. The brothers' younger sister, May Ethel, came to Bidford around 1930 and opened a stylish draper's shop in the High Street, which specialised in baby linen.
37. Bomford and Evershed began life as a limited company and in 1908 moved to Salford Priors. In 1910 they sold their steam cultivation contract work to R and B Bomford and concentrated on rolling, dredging and excavating contracts. The production of ditching and earth moving equipment was only a minor element in the firm's activity until the 'Dig for Victory' campaign during World War 2 made the need for such equipment essential. After the war, the firm began to rely more on manufacturing and in 1967 joined with Bomford Bros to form the Bomford Group.
38. Aveling and Porter were famous agricultural engine and steam roller manufacturers. Thomas Aveling and Richard Porter brought out their first steam engine in 1865 and by the early 20th century were supplying about 70% of the British market for road rollers.
39. Percy Bryan was born in 1890, and, like his father and grandfather before him, became a painter. After serving in the Royal Naval Air Service as an Air Mechanic during the First World War, transferring to the newly-formed RAF in 1918, he returned to Bidford in 1920 to resume his occupation as a painter and carpenter. He was generally acknowledged as 'a super sign writer' and did all the sign writing

for local pubs and businesses. He died in 1949.

40. After the evacuation of the British Expeditionary Force from Dunkirk in 1940, the Government commissioned a new heavy infantry tank to replace the outdated Matilda model. The first Churchill tanks were ready for active service by June 1941 and various design improvements during the next three years led to their becoming the most successful of all British tanks, notable for their ability to climb steep slopes and for their thick protective armour.
41. John Bryan was born in 1861, the son of George and Ann Bryan. He followed in his father's footsteps as a painter and in 1882 married Ann Selina Milward. By 1901 the family had moved to Rose Place, Tower Hill. He died in 1943.
42. William Henry Wilkes was a market gardener before concentrating on dairy farming. In 1939, at the age of 72, he was still running his dairy business assisted by his son, Frederick, and daughters, Daisy and Nellie. He died in 1941.
43. The Fosbroke family's connection with Bidford stretched back over a hundred years and produced three generations of distinguished surgeons. The last of them, George Haynes Fosbroke (1850-1925), was appointed the first Medical Officer of Health for Worcestershire in 1890. He published articles in the British Medical Journal and elsewhere on cancer, diphtheria, copper poisoning and sanitary matters generally. Fosbroke House, the family home, is now a Guest House.
44. This is very probably a reference to Albert Ash, who in 1939 was living on Salford Road with his parents, Edward and Amelia, and three unmarried sisters, and earning his living as a market gardener.
45. A reference to William Smith, recorded in the Trade Directories for 1916-32 as a watchmaker.
46. Fred Holder became one of the more substantial market gardeners in the village. In 1911 he was living in Victoria Road, but by 1916 had moved to the imposing Georgian-style Icknield House in the High Street and in the early thirties built Marleigh House on Waterloo Road. His elevated occupational status is reflected in the 1939 Register where he is described as a Farmer and Fruit Salesman.
47. The rick yard was the place in the farmyard where the hay was commonly stacked. However, the prominence given to Fred Holder's rick yard may be also be linked to its location in Icknield Street, 'Ick' being a corruption of 'Ryk' as in 'Rykneild', 'Ryknild', the ancient Roman Road which ran from the Fosse Way at Bourton-on-the-Water, Gloucestershire to Templeborough in South Yorkshire, and crossed the

River Avon at Bidford.

48. A reference to PC William ('Bill') Mundy.
49. William Henry Cowper (1893-1969) was originally a market gardener and farmer before setting up his coal yard in the High Street. His son, Raymond, carried on the business after Henry's retirement.
50. Charles Dowdeswell was born in 1855. He followed his father and grandfather in the saddlery business and appears in the Trade Directories from 1908-36. He died in 1940.
51. Dr Charles Edward Hobbes (1845-1931) was the second son of Mary Anne Fosbroke and Jonathan Lord Hobbes. He was educated privately at Warwick and in 1861 came to Bidford to assist his uncle, George Haynes Fosbroke, with whom he was later in partnership. After training as a doctor and surgeon, he returned to Bidford in 1874 where he spent the rest of his life in a family practice. He carried out his rounds partly on horseback, partly in a high-wheeled dogcart and gig, then, when the roads improved, by bicycle, and finally by motor car. A keen sportsman, he rode regularly to hounds, successfully competed in horse-jumping events and was a first-rate shot and excellent fisherman. Two or three years before his death, he retired to Broom where he spent his time tending his garden. He married a Miss Scott of Stratford-upon-Avon who survived him.
52. Arguably the most iconic building in Bidford, the Old Falcon dates from the 16th century and during this period was notable for its association with the Shakespeare legend. (See Endnote 18). It was also claimed to be the place where the future king Charles II rallied his troops on their way to the Battle of Worcester in 1651. This is unlikely, however, since Charles and his army approached Worcester from the north, not from the east. Cromwell's main rendezvous, on the other hand, was at Warwick, and it is possible that several county militia regiments that joined him from the south may have crossed the Avon at Bidford. Until the late 18th century the Falcon functioned as an inn and then as the parish workhouse until the Poor Law Act of 1834. In the 1860s it housed the Bidford Institute and Working Men's Reading Room before being converted into a number of private dwellings and shops. By the late 1930s there were five distinct dwellings including an overhanging Elizabethan structure which housed Henrietta Houghton's greengrocery business. This was later demolished to relieve traffic congestion. Today the Falcon building comprises two private houses.

53. Joseph Henry (Harry) Collins (1871-1925) was born in Plymouth. By 1900 he was living in Bidford with his wife, Susan, and their two small children, and had taken over Trenfields' drapery and stationer's business, with Post Office attached. By 1924 it had changed its designation to 'drug store and Post Office'. After his death, his wife carried on the business for a number of years. It was then briefly in the hands of Mrs Susan Rushton, before Jack Griffiths became Postmaster in 1932.
54. The Spiers family was associated with the Bull's Head from the mid-19th century until Fred Spiers' retirement in the 1990s. 'Old Mrs Spiers' refers to Mary Ann Spiers, nee Churchley, (1853-1929), who held the license for over 20 years, before it transferred to her son Alfred in the early 1920s. After Alfred's death in 1934, his wife Victoria took over the license and ran the Bull's Head until her son Fred was old enough to assume responsibility.
55. Noakes and Croft was an upmarket general store which, in addition to groceries, sold hardware, paints, seeds and patent medicines.
56. William Jones (1865-1949) was born in Pebworth. A brickmaker by trade, in 1896 he married Eliza Farr of Bidford, whose father, Frederick, was a local grocer and newsagent. It is clear from a press advertisement that Eliza ran the shop, thus leaving William free to engage in his outdoor activities. In 1911 his occupation is listed as 'Engineer'. After Eliza died in 1930, William took over the running of the shop.
57. The War Memorial was erected in 1923 to commemorate those Bidford men who gave their lives in World War I.
58. Until 1903 the Fisherman's Rest was known as 'The Boot', probably so-named to commemorate the military exploits of the Duke of Wellington. Oral tradition claims that the sign once depicted a Wellington boot.
59. No record of a 'Mrs Edmunds' can be traced. What is known is that by 1924 Arthur Tedd had taken over the sweetshop at Brighton House and by 1939 had extended the business to include general groceries.
60. For over 30 years until his death in 1933, John Gould's butcher's shop was a familiar sight in Bidford High Street.
61. On his death, Edward Joseph Sill (1844-1937) was described as 'Bidford's Grand Old Man'. Born in Worcester, the two year old Edward came to Bidford with his parents, Silvester and Frances. Staunch Roman Catholics, the Sills became one of the most prominent Bidford families during the second half of the 19th century. Edward qualified as a chemist in London before returning to Bidford to take over

his father's grocery business. During the next fifty years, part of the time in partnership with his younger brother, Silvester Junior, he greatly expanded his business interests, becoming a draper, chemist and general dealer, the owner of the brickyard and coal yard (next to Bidford station), a successful farmer, and an agent for Lloyds Bank, Gilbeys, the wine and spirits merchants, and Mr Dent. He and his wife Elizabeth, who died in 1918, had five children. On retiring from business in 1920, he spent the remainder of his life at The Harbour affectionately tending his rose garden.

62. Adjoining the business premises of the Bidford and Mickleton Co-operative Society in the High Street, the Jubilee, or Co-operative Hall, as it was alternatively known, was opened in 1925. It was built by the Co-op to celebrate the Golden Jubilee of the Society's establishment in the village, and although only a wooden structure, it rapidly became more popular than the Assembly Rooms as a venue for dances and other forms of entertainment.
63. For much of the 1920s Ernest Charles Wilkes had his own business as a motor car hirer.
64. James Kendall (1862-1948) was born in Gloucestershire, but moved to Bidford probably in the early 1880s. He and his wife, Eliza Jane, a native of Bidford, produced four sons and three daughters. For much of his working life he was a shoe and boot maker, living in the High Street, but in his later years took up market gardening.
65. A Brougham was a lightweight, enclosed, four-wheeled horse-drawn carriage with two doors which normally seated two people. It had a box seat in front for the coachman and a footman or extra passenger. Its name is derived from the controversial 19th century politician Lord Henry Brougham, who had the carriage built to his own specification.
66. A Landau was a lightweight, four-wheeled horse-drawn carriage with a convertible folded top, which seated four people on two facing seats with an elevated front seat outside the carriage for the coachman. It takes its name from the city of Landau in Germany where it is claimed to have been first produced in the early 18th century. It is still used today on ceremonial occasions such as royal weddings.
67. The business was started in Birmingham at the end of the 19th century by Frederick Lanchester, one of the most influential automobile engineers of his day, and his two brothers, George and Frank. The Lanchester car, first sold to the public in 1901, was one of the first English cars, as opposed to horseless carriages, to be

built, and up to 1914 most cars on the market had Lanchester-built bodies. They were not cheap. One of their models in the 1920s cost more than a Rolls-Royce Silver Ghost. In 1930 the whole of the share capital was sold to BSA.

68. A reference to Rev John Webster Evans, who was vicar of Bidford from 1913 to 1931.
69. The Calthorpe Motor Company, based in Bordesley Green, Birmingham, under the guiding influence of George Hands, made a range of cars, motor cycles and bicycles between 1904 and 1932. The Company was mainly noted for its high-quality, light cars, but by the late 1920s sales of the Calthorpe car were declining and production had virtually ceased by 1928.
70. The Co-op shops during the inter-war period consisted of clothes, grocery and butcher's departments on the ground floor, and a haberdashery department upstairs.
71. James ('Jimmy') William Elsmore (1853-1927) was born in Camden and appears to have come to the Bidford area in the early 1870s. In 1876 he married Annie Davis from Aston Cantlow, but then moved to the Black Country where their five children were born between 1876 and 1886. During the late 1880s he set up a grocery business in Bidford High Street. He died in 1927, but from 1904 until 1940 it is his wife, Annie, 'Grannie' Elsmore as she came to be known, who is listed in the Trade Directories.
72. 'Grubber' was a slang term for 'workhouse'. The latter was also commonly referred to as the 'Spike'.
73. 'Tinker' Wilcox was the nickname of Henry Wilcox (1849-1933) whose ironmonger's shop was a feature of the Bidford landscape for over 50 years.
74. John Davis' baker's shop was a familiar feature in the High Street for over four decades. He was born in Fifield, Oxfordshire, the son of a carpenter and wheelwright, and by 1891 was working as a grocer's assistant at Beckinsale's in Cheltenham. By 1896 he had taken over Job Edginton's baker's shop in the High Street. The same year he married Job's daughter, Mary Ann, who was born in Bidford in 1872. In 1906 John proudly advertised himself as a Baker and Confectioner who held gold medals for White Bread and for Hovis Bread and Confectionery, awarded by the Master Bakers' Society. He died in 1938.
75. James Newman Gray (1855-1938) established a drapery business in Bidford in the late 19th century. By 1921 the firm had changed its name to Gray and Friend, Charles Friend and his wife Annie taking over the running of the shop until Charles' death in 1934.

76. Born in the adjacent parish of Salford Priors in 1875, George Winnett had a butcher's shop in Bidford High Street for over 30 years. In 1911, apart from his wife and four children, he housed three butcher's assistants and a domestic servant. Not surprisingly, he advertised his business as 'the largest butcher's in Bidford'.
77. Frederick Joseph ('Joe') Prickett (1886-1956) rose from being a 'butcher manager' in 1911 to the status of 'master butcher' in 1939.
78. The name 'Mason's Arms' reflects the importance of stonemasons in the village economy up to the mid-20th century, not only those who worked in the building trade but also those who quarried the local blue lias stone. Several publicans during the late 18th and 19th centuries were also masons, suggesting that during the period the Mason's Arms was very much the masons' pub. For over 30 years from the 1890s, the license was held by the Holder family. In the 1960s the pub was renamed the Anglo-Saxon, after the adjacent Anglo-Saxon burial ground excavated in the 1920s, and an implicit recognition that stonemasons by then represented a less significant element in the Bidford workforce.
79. As his nickname suggests, William John Bennett was a hairdresser. He started his business early in the century and continued throughout the inter-war period. His wife, Gertrude, sold haberdashery in the main shop while William was busy cutting men's hair in a room at the back and playing his violin between customers.
80. Dents are famous the world over for their high quality leather goods. Founded in 1777 by John Dent of Worcester, the firm is still in business today.
81. John Barlow was landlord of the White Lion Hotel from 1877 until his death in 1895. He was an able and ambitious man who is generally credited with 'putting Bidford on the map' by advertising its attractions to a wider public and turning the White Lion into one of the most noted inns in the region. In 1884 he designated the largest room in the hotel as an Assembly Room in an attempt to raise the status of the establishment, and in 1893 opened the three-storey Assembly Rooms in the High Street which were not demolished until 1967.
82. See Endnote 14.
83. A reference to the 16th century manor house at Gorcott near Redditch which from 1958 became Skilts School, the last of Birmingham's Open Air Schools to be built for Birmingham children suffering from a range of respiratory conditions and also for those experiencing social and emotional problems. Today it operates as a Residential Special School for Primary age boys.

84. William Gardner (1871-1932) was the landlord of the Fisherman's Rest public house from the beginning of the century until his death, as well as running a thriving osier business for much of this period. He married his first wife, Caroline, in 1894 and, following her death, married Miriam Rimell (1860-1951), better known as 'Minnie', in 1913. After William's death, Minnie, who had a reputation for being 'quite fierce' and swearing 'like a trooper' took over as licensee of the Fisherman's Rest for a few years.
85. The Trade Directory for 1928 lists a 'John Denness' as proprietor of the White Lion. 'Arthur Denness' is not mentioned, but it can be reasonably assumed that Jack Moore is referring to this period of the mid/late 1920s. The link with motorised transport may be reflected in the mention in the 1924 Directory of Denness & Co Ltd as motor repairers.
86. Referred to as 'Bellyncourt' in 1500, Bell Court was the home of Albert Edward Bailey and his family for nearly 20 years during the first quarter of the 20th century. One of his six daughters, Barbara (born 1907), became well-known in later life as the author Barbara Comyns. Her first book, *Sisters by a River*, published in 1947, is an entertaining, if somewhat surreal, account of her childhood in Bidford, seen through the eyes of the child.
87. Crossley was a pioneering company in the production and development of internal combustion engines. The Crossley brothers, Francis and William, began the business in 1867 in the centre of Manchester before moving to larger premises in Openshaw in 1881. Realising that the future lay with new gas fuelled atmospheric internal combustion engines and the heavier oil fuelled engines, the company continued to expand and also became involved in the development of diesel and petrol engines. Their notable organisational innovation, the production line, attracted a visit to Openshaw from none other than Henry Ford. The company made over 100,000 Crossley oil and gas engines, a few of which are still in use today.
88. A reference to Annie Lea (1870-1936). After her husband Job, a tailor, died in 1916, Annie kept her tobacconist's shop throughout the 1920s. During the following decade she handed over the running of the shop to her daughter Cicely, in order to turn her home into a boarding house.
89. The Pleasure Grounds were established by William Murrell Holland at the beginning of the century, when he was described in the 1901 Census as 'Steam launch and boat proprietor'. In the 1912 Directory this description had changed to

'Refreshment rooms', a term which continued through to 1940. After his father's death in 1921, William Henry Holland, 'Daddy Holland', as he was known, took over the business. The Pleasure Grounds were laid out in a delightful garden setting bordering the River Avon. Steamer and boat trips were popular; punts were available for hire and children could enjoy the swing boats and roundabouts. A tea shop, managed by Daddy Holland's two sisters, was not the least of the varied attractions.

90. The Blackwell family had been associated with Bickmarsh Hall since the 1870s. Samuel Fowler Blackwell (1861-1907) formed the company, S F Blackwell Ltd, and by 1881 was farming 1,000 acres, employing 25 men, 5 women and 10 boys. In 1921, when it was owned by George Blackwell Sims, the acreage had grown to 2,000 acres and the workforce to between 60 and 70 labourers. The estate was notable for the variety of agriculture carried out. Market garden crops in the form of fruit and vegetables took their place alongside cereals, hay and largescale livestock breeding. Two 14 hp. Fowler steam ploughs and four motor tractors were employed in addition to more traditional horse-drawn machinery. See also *Almanac* Introduction p.9.
91. A lightweight, normally horse-drawn, hand plough.
92. The narrow track between the churchyard and the cemetery leading down to the River Avon is thought to have been one of three crossing points in Roman and Saxon times. The origin of the name is uncertain, possibly a corruption of 'dove house', but often referred to locally as 'Duffers'. During the inter-war years, the Avon below Duffus Lane was a popular swimming place for children since the river at that point was relatively shallow.
93. The existence of what must have been a water-driven corn mill is first recorded in Domesday Book. With the advance of technology in the 19th century, 'Roller Mills' increasingly replaced the traditional 'grist' mill. As the name suggests, they used cylindrical rollers to crush the grain, often in opposing pairs. The Broom roller mills were part of a mid-19th construction with late century additions. In 1896 the mill was owned by John Atkins and then from 1916 by Atkins and Thomas Ltd. It provided a steady source of employment for local people until its closure in the late-1980s.
94. The 'Four Alls' is a name given to various pubs across the country, for example, in the village of Higham in the heart of 'Pendle Witch' country, where a supposed curse was put on the ale and the landlord's son was enchanted. The name 'Four

Alls' stands for:

1. The King rules all
2. The Priest prays for all
3. The Soldier fights for all
4. The Ordinary man pays for all.

The Welford pub is located by the Binton bridges just off the main Evesham to Stratford Road on the outskirts of Welford village.

95. A reference to Bidford High School which opened in April 1938 when 118 children were admitted. Throughout the forties and fifties the School received very good reports from HM Inspectors, and remained popular with parents and pupils alike until its controversial closure by the County Council in 1985.

96. The name Marriage Hill is popularly thought to have originated from 'marl ridge', but an alternative view suggests it may have derived from the Old English 'maer-hrycg' meaning 'boundary ridge', since it is very close to the boundary between the parishes of Bidford-on-Avon and Salford Priors.

97. In October 1901 a bridge was built over the River Arrow, thereby facilitating links with Dunnington. The Jam factory appears to have opened during the early years of the 20th century. The original factory was built of timber and corrugated tin sheets on the site by the river known as Tinkers Close. There is some evidence to suggest that loads of fruit from the factory were transported by horse and cart to the fruit processing and bottling factory in Dunnington, on the site of 'Hillers' today. A photograph taken during the First World War shows a factory staff of at least 30, mainly women, but little is yet known about the factory's ownership and management. For a number of years the factory's 'Jamite' Band was a feature of village musical life, notably when it led the procession in Bidford to mark the conclusion of the Armistice in November 1918. During World War I the Ministry of Agriculture and Fisheries erected additional buildings on the site, and in 1921 the land and buildings were sold to Mr Adkins of Broom Mill. The Factory closed sometime during the 1920s, but for a period thereafter the building was used as the village hall where organisations such as the Women's Institute held their meetings. Although the original structure proved remarkably durable, by the mid-1970s the tin sheets had become dangerously loose and the building was demolished in 1977. Thereafter, the site was leased to a succession of businesses before giving way to a modern housing development.

98. Born in Bidford in 1854, Henry ('Harry') Mason was the Broom blacksmith for over 50 years. He is first listed as a blacksmith in the 1881 Census when he was in lodgings in Broom. Later that year he married Annie Harris, a dressmaker, from Kempsey in Worcestershire. They had four daughters, two of whom became schoolteachers, one a dressmaker and one a music teacher. Harry died, two years after his wife, in 1932.
99. In reality, 'Bother'em Dick' was one William Edwin Bryan, who was born in Arrow in 1863 and died in Bidford in 1937. He worked as a water diviner and well sinker. The nickname emanates from his habit of hiding in the Lych Gate of the Church and leaping out on passers-by as a joke. He was also known as someone who knocked on people's doors and bothered them for any unwanted items. He died in his home at 9 Victoria Road and when the new owners moved in, they discovered the house and garden to be full of the items he had collected over the years. He also promised that if the house did not remain in the Bryan family, he would come back and haunt it. The house is no longer occupied by a Bryan family member, but the current owners have experienced no such ghostly encounter.
100. A family of wharfingers, the Hendleys, appear to have been the first landlords of the public house in the mid-19th century. The 1861Census refers to George Hendley as a coal merchant and innkeeper at the 'coal wharf and public house' and a few years later, a document relating to his estate mentions the Boat Inn Wharf, implying that originally the inn catered predominantly for commercial boatmen. His wife Betsy took over as licensee, and within a year had renamed the pub, the 'Pleasure Boat', reflecting the increasing number of pleasure craft on the river and the fact that by this time the Avon was rarely being used for the transporting of heavy materials such as coal. The entry in the 1896 Trade Directory claimed: 'every description of boat built to order... first class fleet of boats for hire; good accommodation for cyclists and parties'. During the late 1870s and 1880s, the Pleasure Boat was a regular meeting place for members of the newly formed National Agricultural Workers Union. In the late 20th century the pub changed its name to the Frog and Bullrush and, more recently still, to The Frog.
101. Dating from the late 16th century, and undergoing extensive alteration during the Victorian period, Broom Hall was originally a farmstead. During the 1920s it was a private dwelling, but by 1940 had been converted into a private hotel and is today a popular inn restaurant.

102. This refers to Lewis Willoughby Nash who was born in Winchcombe in 1914. His mother married Frederick Taylor, a market gardener, in 1919 and they lived on Tower Hill, Bidford. Given their fathers' profession, it is likely that Jack Moore would have known Lewis quite well. When World War II was declared, Lewis joined the Leicestershire Regiment as a Private before transferring to the Intelligence Corps. He was taken prisoner when Singapore fell to the Japanese on 15th February 1942 and was taken to Camp M464 at Chungkai in Thailand to work on the infamous Death Railway. Conditions were awful and he died on the last day of September, 1943, aged 29. He is buried in Chungkai war cemetery, Chungkai was one of the base camps on the railway and contained a hospital and church built by Allied prisoners of war, who also began the work on the war cemetery.
103. Elijah Bryan (1862-1941) started work as an agricultural labourer. In 1881 he was living with his widowed mother, Elizabeth, whose occupation was that of glove maker. He married Emma Hendley in 1890 and by the following year was employed as a grocer's carter. Although he was officially listed as 'carrier' to Stratford-upon-Avon and Evesham for much of the 1920s and 1930s, he declined to use motor vehicles and continued to use a horse and cart as his means of transport throughout this period.
104. Not to be confused with the Big Meadow, Money Meadow was a field on the eastern side of Bidford Bridge where the annual fair was held and 'money' was made.
105. A severe 60 mile course for motor cyclists through the Cotswold Hills from Stratford-upon-Avon to Winchcombe, dating back to 1917.
106. Born in Cleeve Prior in 1860, John Collett married Ellen Thornton of Bidford in 1879. By 1881 they were living on Tower Hill and his recorded occupation until 1911 was that of labourer. It is not clear at what time he took on the role of gravedigger, but he may have combined this with other labouring tasks.
107. 'Grange' was a term used to describe the area eastwards beyond the village bordering the Avon. It took its name from the medieval manor of Bidford Grange, which before the Dissolution of the Monasteries, belonged to the Abbots of Bordesley. In the early 20th century, it was one of the largest farms in the district.
108. James Thomas ('Tommy') Hope was born in Colwall near Ledbury in 1855 and was still living there in 1871. How and where he met his wife, Marianne, is unclear, but they married in Droitwich in 1877. In 1881 the couple were living in West

Street, Stratford-upon-Avon, and Thomas was established as a hairdresser. By 1891 Marianne had born him five children. She died in 1898.

109. All but one of the Comics listed were published by Alfred Harmsworth's Amalgamated Press. *Illustrated Chips*, published between 1890 and 1953, featured tramps Weary Willie and Tired Tim, and the Nibs from Casey Court, led by the larger-than-life Billy Baggs. *Comic Cuts* was published from 1890-1953, The *Rainbow* from 1914 to 1956, and *Tiger Tim and Friends* from 1919 to 1940 when it merged with the *Rainbow*. *The Gem* (1907-39) was a story paper mainly featuring the boys at the fictional school, St. Jim's. The majority of the stories were written by Charles Hamilton, better known as Frank Richards, the creator of Billy Bunter of Greyfriars, who appeared in *The Magnet*, a story comic which ran from 1908 to 1940. The one exception to the Harmsworth monopoly was *Boys' Own*, which was first published in 1879 by the Religious Tract Society. It aimed to instil Christian morals into young children during their formative years and unashamedly promoted the British Empire as the highest achievement of civilisation.

110. The Davis family had a stonemason's business in Bidford for over 100 years. In Jack Moore's time the head of the business was William Henry Davis (1860-1935) whose status in the village community was underlined by his position as Assistant Overseer of the Poor for nearly 30 years. He also served as Parish Clerk for a short period.

111. The counties concerned were Warwickshire, Worcestershire and Gloucestershire.

112. Its origin is obscure. The name appears on an undated map around 1870 and on the first edition of the 6 inch Ordnance Survey map of 1883. The most likely, though not proven, explanation is that it refers to a dwelling occupied by a migrating Welshman who settled there possibly several centuries before. What is clear is that it was situated on a well-used trackway running west to east. The poet, publisher and conservationist, Felix Dennis, who took over the Old Manor in Dorsington and renewed over a thousand acres of woodland, helped to keep the name alive by restoring an old barn which he called the Welshman's Barn.

113. Once a medieval manor house, Clay Hall was the home of the Fulwood (Fulwode) family. The first recorded mention of Clay Hall is 1396, but a manor house is known to have existed during the reign of Henry II. The building is long since demolished, no trace of it is visible above ground and there are doubts as to its exact location.

114. School Attendance Officers have their origin in the 1870 Education Act which sought to make education available to all children, but it was the Act of 1881 making education compulsory for all five to ten year olds that established Attendance Officers as key instruments in enforcing the legislation. If they ignored the warnings given by Attendance Officers, parents could be prosecuted for failing to ensure that their children attend school. During the early 20th century, as more understanding of the underlying economic causes of non-attendance increased, prosecutions began to decline and Attendance Officers gradually assumed more of a welfare role.The men appointed to the post often had a background in the armed forces or had held previous positions of authority in the workplace. Thomas ('Bobby') Lester (1857-1940) was no exception. He was born in Warwick and for a number of years worked as a warehouse foreman in a gelatine factory in the city before moving to Alcester sometime after 1901. The School Log Books record visits as Attendance Officer to Bidford Infant and Junior Schools from 1913 onwards. He retired in 1925 at the age of 67 and spent the remainder of his life in Alcester with his wife, Sarah Anne.
115. Born in 1893, John Osborne was the son of John and Caroline Osborne of California Cottage. He was not the only member of the large Osborne family to have been employed as a Telegraph Messenger. Albert William Osborne was described as such in the 1911 Census.
116. Wilson's funfairs of Redditch were a familiar sight at Bidford Carnivals and festivals during the 20th century. The family's involvement in funfairs dates back at least 200 years, making them one of the oldest family firms in the business. Ginny Horse roundabouts were merry-go-rounds with standing horses, always one of the most popular attractions at such fairs.
117. A reference to the stretch of road from the eastern end of Mill Lane in Broom to the junction with the Bidford to Wixford road. The origin of the name is unclear, though it may be a reference to the time before the road was properly made up.
118. The Lanes were a farming family who resided at Broom Court from the early 19th century to the early 1930s when John Lane and his wife Edith removed to live at The Woodloes in Warwick.
119. Probably a reference to Sidney Smith Slaughter (1901-1966), the son of Walter Charles and Ann Slaughter. His father was a pork butcher before taking up market gardening in Marlcliff and Sidney appears to have followed a similar

path. For much of the 1920s he had a pork butcher's shop in Bidford, but by 1939 he was living at Oaklands in Victoria Road and listed as a self-employed market gardener.

120. Caroline (1853-1937) married John Osborne (1847-1919) in 1871 and very possibly moved in to California Cottage soon afterwards. In 1881 their family consisted of four daughters and one son. By 1891 Caroline had produced three more daughters, and a further four sons were added to the family during the next ten years. (see endnote 115) During this period John's employment varied between general labouring and plate laying on the nearby Stratford and Midland Junction Railway.

121. George Moore (1858-1928) and his wife Martha had at least 11 children. He was employed as a blacksmith on the Bickmarsh estate for more than half his working life. By 1911 he had moved from south of the River Avon to live in Victoria Road, Bidford, where he spent the remaining years of his life.

122. John Henry Allen (1858-1937) was one of an expanding type of agricultural worker in the early 20th century, having being trained as a driver of steam engines and steam ploughs.

123. Arthur Whiting (1873-1944) was born in Gloucestershire. In 1893 he married Florence Showell and for many years they lived in Westbury-on-Severn, the birthplace of most of their 16 children. In 1911 Arthur's occupation was recorded as 'Machinist Corn Thrashing'. It is perhaps not surprising that he was skilled in a variety of country crafts, since threshing was a seasonal task. His grand-daughter recalls that when he and his growing family moved to Bidford, the reasons for which are unclear, they carried their furniture on a horse-drawn cart. They settled in Icknield Street, Arthur being listed as a Farm Labourer in 1939.

124. In the Trade Directories for 1908 to 1936 Charles Harris is described as an oil merchant. He lived for much of this time in Alcester Road, Bidford with his wife, Agnes, and daughter, Sophie. The Wesleyan Methodist chapel at the top of Chapel Alley was built in 1804 and enlarged in 1837.

125. The name cannot be traced on contemporary maps. It is possibly a shortened form of Primrose Hill.

126. Probably the John Tarver listed in the 1911 Census as living in Broom with his wife, Kate, and employed as an agricultural labourer. He died in 1939.

127. No Creswells can be traced in Bidford during this period. There were Creswells living in Harvington, just across the county boundary in Worcestershire and others

in the Evesham area, but none identified as 'thatchers'. It is possible that some of them combined thatching with their recorded occupations of 'garden labourer' or 'market gardener'.

128. 'Johnny on the Mopstick' was a variation on the age-old game of 'Buck Buck' which involved one group of players climbing on the backs of another with the aim of building as high a pile as possible or causing the supporting players to collapse. There were many regional variations. In Birmingham the game went under the name of 'Polly on the Mopstick' and in East London it was known as 'High Jimmy Knacker'. It could also be found in Europe: as early as the mid-16th century children are depicted playing a version of the game in Pieter Bruegel's painting *Children's Games.*
129. This observation was confirmed by Dorothy Johnson, who remembers having whooping cough at a time when the lane was being tarred, and Dr Murray telling her mother: 'Go and stand by the tar machine and tell her to breathe in and out'.
130. Almost certainly a reference to the carpenter Charles Stanley (1855-1928) of Broom. His son, Ernest Charles (born 1884), followed his father in the carpentry trade and part of his work, according to oral testimony, involved making coffins.
131. 'Stanley Nailor, fishmonger, High Street' is listed in the Trade Directory for 1928. His tenure appears to have been of relatively short duration, most of his working life having been spent in the Evesham area. In 1911 he was working as an assistant fishmonger in a shop in Evesham High Street and by 1939 had set up in business as a fishmonger and fruiterer in North Littleton.

GLOSSARY

The items listed are italicised in the *Almanac* text:

Backband
a broad leather strap passing over the horse's back to support the long chains of trace harness.

Baffle plates
a device used in this instance to regulate or restrain the flow of water.

Bagging hook
a hand-held tool with a curved blade, similar to a sickle but heavier, and typically used for harvesting or reaping grain crops.

Barmed
fermented. 'Barm' was commonly a term for 'yeast'.

Baulks
roughly squared timber beams.

Belle de Louvain ('Belle d'vain')
a large purple plum, originating in Belgium in the mid-19th century. Its hardy nature enables it to grow in cold and windy conditions and to be resistant to disease. In cooking its dry flesh prevents pastry and tarts from going soggy, but it also makes delicious jam.

Billhook
alternatively known as 'billock' or 'hedge bill', the billhook was a traditional short, wooden-handled cutting tool with a long iron blade and hooked tip. It was used widely in forestry and agriculture for cutting shrubs and branches, but especially in trimming and laying hedges.

Blenheim
Blenheim Orange, otherwise known as 'Dempster's Pippin', is a cultivar of apple, and is noted for its vigorous cropping. It was discovered around 1740 at Woodstock, near to Blenheim Palace, and can be used both as a cooking apple and for dessert.

Boltings
the coarse particles separated from the grain by sifting.

Bout
a stint or set task, sometimes denoting a day's work.

Butt
the base of the bush or tree especially that just above the ground.

Carborundum
a hard black solid containing silicon carbide, used as an abrasive.

Carvel-built
unlike clinker-built boats where the wooden planks of the hull overlap along their edges, carvel planks are fixed to frames with their edges butting up against each other with no overlap and thus forming a smooth surface.

Chaff
the protective casing or husks of grain, separated from the grain by winnowing or threshing and then cut into small pieces by a chaff cutter, mixed with other forage and fed to horses and cattle.
See also:
Threshing and Winnowing.

Chain harrows
one of a number of harrow types, chain harrows are used to aerate grassland or to cover freshly-sown seed.

Chawl
a cut of pork meat from the fleshier lower cheeks and lower jaw of the pig's head.

Chitted
another term for 'sprouted', often used of potatoes.

Chitterlings
the small intestines of pigs which are then prepared, often fried, for human consumption.

Cocks
short for 'haycocks', which were conically stacked piles of hay.

Cordwood
wood cut into uniform short lengths and used especially for firewood or for building purposes.

Crock (crook)
the bend in the tool near the handle.

Crow Onions
otherwise known as 'crow's poison'. Mildly toxic, they look almost identical to small wild onions, but, whereas the onion smells like onion when crushed, crow onions smell more like grass.

Cruppers
leather straps attached to the back of a saddle and looped under the horse's tail to prevent the saddle or harness from slipping forward.

Cure-All Five Oils
one of several oil-based treatments for horse ailments and diseases.

Curry comb
a tool made of rubber or plastic with short 'teeth' on one side. Usually the first tool used in horse grooming. The horse is rubbed or 'curried' in a circular motion to help loosen dirt, hair and other detritus and stimulate the skin to produce natural oils.

Dabchicks
the nickname for 'little grebes'.

Dandy brush
a stiff-bristled brush used on a horse to remove dirt, hair stirred up by the curry comb. Normally applied in short strokes from front to back, except at the flanks where the hair grows in a different pattern.

Ditching grout
a form of cement used to strengthen the side of the ditch side against collapse. See also **Grouts**.

'Dog and Stick' farming
a phrase denoting low input, low output farming, often used to describe the period after World War I when arable crops were in decline and greater emphasis was being placed on the rearing of livestock. 'Dog and stick' represent the minimal tools required for such low investment agriculture.

Dog-irons
the term 'dog-irons' normally refers to the supports which raise a fire grate. In this case, however, the metal tyres rested on fire-bricks and the dog irons are 'dogs' or iron rods (with a hooked end), used as levers.

Dray
a flat-bed, long-sided, four-wheeled vehicle, strong

enough to carry heavy goods and used on both roads and farms.

Drift

a strip or line from one end of a field to another.

Egg Plum/Pershore Egg: a good quality yellow plum, used particularly for cooking, it is extensively grown in the Vale of Evesham, one of the most popular varieties being Pershore Yellow.

Espalier

a space-saving method of growing fruit on a wall or fence. Once established, the fruit requires little pruning and when in blossom and in fruit is attractive to look at.

Fagging hook

similar to a bagging hook, a small hooked scythe-like tool with sharp blades which are heavier and wider than those of the sickle. The reaper would hold back the stalks or draw them towards him with a fagging stick and then slash through the straw with the fagging hook in one sharp action rather than saw through the straw as with a sickle. In this way, a larger quantity of corn was cut at one swing.

Fellies

the outer rim of a wheel to which the spokes are fixed.

Fordraft

a West Midlands dialect term for a 'lane', sometimes 'foredraft'.

Foremost/Fillers

fillers are the horses or oxen behind the foremost animals in heavy plough teams.

Frog

part of the underside of a horse's hoof. Triangular in shape, it extends midway from the heel towards the toe. It acts as a shock absorber for the foot when it makes contact with the ground, thus lessening the force placed on the bones and joints.

Gillies

Wallflowers, otherwise known as 'gillyflowers'.

G.O. Lines

term used to denote a pair of cord reins. Horses reacted to the first sound of command such as 'Goo orn', when the reins were clicked to get them moving. The shout 'Whoa' was commonly used to order them to stop.

'Gone Away'

a huntsman's cry, indicating that a fox has been started, the hounds are in full cry and the hunt is on.

Governors

a device on a steam or stationary engine that controls its speed, regardless of load, when it is powering another machine.

Grouts

in this context, holes or trenches dug to pass the chains through. It may be a variation of a local dialect word, 'gowt', meaning 'a short drain' [Jesse Salisbury: 'South East Worcestershire Words and Phrases', 1893].

Gunwale

pronounced 'gunnel', the reinforced upper edge of a boat. The name originally meant 'gun plank' and referred to that part of the deck where the guns were mounted.

Hames

two curved pieces of metal or wood attached to the front of a draught horse's collar, and through which the horse supplies power.

Haysel

haymaking, or more specifically, the season for making hay.

Hearthstoning

a hearthstone was a flat soft stone used to whiten or scour hearths, steps, floors etc.

Headland
the area at each end of a planted field which was used for turning around farm horses and implements.
'Haddlelun' was a local variation on a very old dialect word for 'headland', regularly referred to in Fred Archer's books on the Vale of Evesham as 'addledum' and in John Clare's 'The Shepherd's Calendar' (1827) as 'Edding'.
Heatherings
a term referring to the bindings, often made from hazel, which are used in hedge-laying. In the Midland style, after stakes have been driven into the ground at regular intervals to help provide firmness to the hedge, three bindings are wound together around the stakes and the tops of the stems which form the hedge's horizontal layers.
Herden
a coarse fabric made from refuse flax or hemp.
Hooving
a dialect term for 'hoeing' in Warwickshire and Worcestershire. A hoeing 'plate' is now more commonly known as a 'blade'
Kettle hangers
sticks of about one inch in diameter with a straight leg and a branch from which a kettle or pot could be hung.
Laird pens
derived from the terms 'lair' and 'lairage', denoting an enclosure for farm animals, especially those earmarked for slaughter.
Lax it down
loosen, break up the clay.
Leaf for lard
leaf lard is the highest known grade of lard, obtained from the soft fat around the kidneys and loin of the pig. It has little pork flavour, but is good for making flaky pie crusts.
Leather bends
a 'bend' is a softish leather made from that part of cattle hide, known as the 'butt', which was left after the belly and shoulder had been removed.
Left proud
sticking out'.
Lights
lungs.
Mangolds
or 'Mangold-wurzels, a variety of beet grown as cattle food.
Mattock
a long-handled agricultural tool similar to a pick-axe, used for digging and loosening the soil.
Martingale
a strap or set of straps running from the noseband or reins to the girth of a horse, used to stop the horse from raising its head too high.
Mauling
an old dialect word meaning 'toiling'.
Mawkins
a dialect word for 'scarecrow'.
Molly hearns
a local dialect term for 'herons'. Fred Archer refers to 'mull herns'.
Morello
a traditional English cooking cherry, one of the best varieties for making cherry pies and jam. It can be eaten fresh when very ripe, but Morello belongs to the acid / sour cherry species rather than the sweeter varieties which are generally preferred for eating straight from the tree.
Neatsfoot Oil
a yellow oil derived and purified from cows' shin bones

and feet. 'Neat' comes from an Old English word for 'cattle'. The oil is used as a conditioning, softening and preservative agent for leather.

Old man's beard
a vigorous and prolific climbing plant, otherwise known as 'wild clematis' or 'traveller's joy', which in autumn and winter is covered in fluffy white seed heads.

Osiernates
osier beds. Once cut, the osiers were then floated downstream to the rod works where they were peeled, bundled together and then transported by lorry to Birmingham or wherever they were to be made into wicker baskets or cradles.

Pershore Egg: see Egg Plum

Piece
an old term to denote a portion of land, as in 'Steppes Piece' (Bidford-on-Avon), Hawkes Piece (Harvington, Worcs).

Pig chats
left overs given to pigs.

Pikle fork
commonly a pitch fork, very similar to a 'shuppick fork'.

Pitching hole
a space for a man to stand in about half way up the haystack, to whom the bale of hay was thrown from below. He would catch it on his pitch-fork and throw it on to the ricker at the top of the stack. An experienced pitcher would catch it on the rise and speed it up on its way. When the rick was completed, the pitching hole would be filled in.

Pitsaw
a large saw with handles at the top and bottom used in a vertical position by two men, one standing above the timber or stone to be cut, the other in the pit below it.

Pole
alternatively 'rod' or 'perch'. A unit of length equal to five and a half yards, commonly used as a unit of measurement before the introduction of the metric system.

Pole gearing
refers to a single wooden shaft ('pole') to which a pair of horses can be yoked and harnessed ('geared').

Pot hampers
square baskets with a cover, usually made from withies. They were ideal containers for fruit and vegetables, especially asparagus. Hampers came in different sizes for marketing purposes, and upturned empty hampers were regularly used for sitting on during work breaks.

Race
a strong or rapid current of water flowing through a narrow channel to drive the mill wheel.

Ratchet
a bar or wheel with a set of angled teeth in which a cog or tooth engages to ensure motion in one direction only.

Ratted
the term suggests 'fringed by fraying or combing' as in contemporary speech: 'ratted jean', deliberately frayed; or 'ratted hair', with split ends.

Rebeading
reseating a bead on a tyre. The 'bead' is the edge of the tyre that sits on the wheel. Wheels for cars, carts, cycles etc are made with a small slot or groove in which the tyre bead sits. When the tyre is fully inflated, the air pressure within the tyre keeps the bead in the groove.

Ridge horse-chains
the ridger, or back chain, supports the shafts of a cart, wagon or dray. The chain sits in a channel in the cart saddle on the horse's back, and takes some of the weight

of the vehicle and its balanced load. The term 'ridge chain' was commonly applied to 'ridge and furrow' ploughing. According to Pip Handy, when ploughing 'ridge and furrow', it was normal for the smaller horse to be placed on the ridge and the larger horse in the furrow, the horses linked by cross chains which kept them together.

Rivers' Early Prolific
a very heavy cropping, quite small early season plum with very dark blue fruits, named after the nursery in Sawbridgeworth, Hertfordshire where it was first raised in the 1820s.

Rocking riddle
a type of large sieve.

Rolling flutes
fluted rollers forming the end part of the sieving mechanism in a threshing drum.

Rope-walk
a long narrow shed, alley or flat piece of ground where strands of material, such as yarns and fibres, are laid out before being twisted into rope.

Routing
in the case of pigs, grubbing up the ground with their snout in search of food.

Rowing man
the man who raked the hay into rows, a process known as 'rowing up'.

Sails
the rotors that drove the corn over the blades.

Saw pit
see '**pitsaw**'.

Scions
a detached part of a plant capable of propagating, especially by grafting.

Score
20 or 21 pounds in weight.

Scotched
a dialect term for 'wedged'.

Scratting box, or 'scratter'
a machine used in cidermaking to crush apples and pears before the pressing extracts the juice.

Scuffling
another term for 'scarifying'.

Sharps and Middlings
both were waste by-products of the milling process. Sharps derived from an earlier stage in the process than middlings. As a result they contained more fibre and were coarser in texture. Middlings were made up of the innermost layers removed from the wheat grain in the making of flour and much resembled flour in character. Sharps and middlings were mainly used to feed pigs and poultry.

Shell-board
a mould-board, that part of a plough which turns aside the earth as it is cut by the coulter.

Shoddy
cloth of inferior quality; term used in the woollen trade for waste from the carding machine or a term for any rotten substance.

Shrove or 'shreave' ladders
ladders with extended ends which were placed on the hay wagon. 'Shreave' is one of several dialect spellings.

Shuppick fork
a local term, especially in Herefordshire and Gloucestershire, for a hay-fork or two-pronged fork, more commonly known as a pitchfork.

Shut in
a term often used in Worcestershire denoting putting a

horse in the shafts, and thus implying work can now begin.

Shut off

removing the horse from the shafts, so that it can rest from its labours.

Siding

a term to denote part of a field (often the 'side') where ploughing was more difficult and additional horse-power was sometimes required.

Skid pan

an iron shoe or clog attached to a chain which was placed under the wheel of a wagon to prevent it from turning when descending a steep hill.

Sledges

Sledge hammers.

Staddle stones

they were mushroom-shaped, made up of a base stone, which tapered towards the top, and an overlapping cap stone. They were used as a supporting base for granaries and hayricks. The stones lifted the granaries and hayricks above the ground thereby keeping the stored grain dry and protecting it from rats and other vermin.

Stank

an old Midland dialect word to denote a small dam.

Stay

a short prop or support.

Steer

a male bovine animal, less than four years old, which has been castrated before sexual maturity.

Stooking

bundling several sheaves of corn.

Store cattle

cattle that are not quite ready for slaughter, often between 15 and 18 months old. They are 'stored' over the winter on a forage diet to keep them growing before being 'finished' on grass the following summer,

Swatheboard or 'swath board'

a slanting board attached to the outer end of the cutter bar of a mower to force the cut grass into a narrower 'swath' so as to leave a cleared strip for the mower wheel when cutting the next swath. A 'swath' refers to the row of cut grass or grain left by a scythe or mowing machine.

Swingletree, or 'whippletree'

a wooden or metal crossbar, pivoted in the centre, to which the draught chains from the horse are attached when undertaking ploughing or other field work, the function of the swingletree being to balance the pull of a horse from alternate shoulders as the animal walks.

Tanglefoot

a frequently used term to denote a rather strong type of intoxicating liquor, in this case home-made parsnip wine. In the US whisky was described as 'tanglefoot'. The term may have originated from as early as the late 18th century when John Woodhouse, the Head Brewer of the brewery firm, Hall and Woodhouse, invited his team to sample his latest brew. Woodhouse was accompanied by his dog who, when his master rose to go, thought a walk was imminent and in his excitement tangled him up in the lead. This apparently gave Woodhouse the idea to call his new beer 'Tanglefoot'. The company still markets 'Tanglefoot' which sells as a golden ale with flavours of melon and pear.

Teasels

tall wildflower plants with thorns all the way up their stems. Their rosy-purple thistle-like flowers and ripening seed heads are a great attraction for bees and goldfinches.

Threshing and Winnowing

threshing is the process by which the edible part of

cereal grain is loosened from the inedible surrounding chaff. It takes place after harvesting and before winnowing. Winnowing is the process by which the loosened chaff is separated from the grain, either manually by beating with a flail or mechanically by the action of a threshing machine.

Tine

the slender pointed projecting part or prong of a fork.

Trace horses

a 'trace' is one of two or more straps, ropes or chains by which a cart or wagon is drawn by a harness horse or other draught animal. A 'trace horse' is one coupled in front of another horse, either as a help for a shaft horse to pull a laden cart or wagon, or when ploughing heavy land and walking in line down the furrow. When a misbehaving trace horse steps outside the long chains attaching it to the load it could be said to be 'kicking over the traces'.

Tracing

a dialect word meaning 'following' or 'tracking' the river somewhat aimlessly.

Traveller

a device used by wheelwrights and blacksmiths to measure the circumference of a wooden wheel before it is fitted with a metal tyre.

Trussing machine

'trussing' is the operation of binding hay cut from the rick for more convenient transportation. The hay was cut into cubic blocks with a hay-knife to a certain weight, the precise weight of the truss varying from region to region. It was then tied by a hay-rope passing once across each of its sides. The invention of the trussing machine in the early 19th century speeded up the binding process and made the weighing more uniform.

Twist

a twisted roll of tobacco.

Victoria

a plum with red or mottled skin, named after Queen Victoria and one of the most common and popular plum varieties.

Walleys

the lines into which hay is raked before being carted or made into heaps or 'cocks'.

Warwickshire Drooper

an old variety of plum that originated in the West Midlands. So-called after its tendency to droop, it has large yellow fruits speckled red with yellow juicy flesh. Strong growing, it crops regularly and heavily.

William

the William 'Bon Chretien' pear, commonly known as the Williams pear (or the Bartlett pear in the US), is the most widely grown pear in the western world. Pleasantly flavoured, its initially green skin turns a golden colour on ripening. It is good for cooking and also for eating. The name 'bon chretien' was a creation of the Italians, who in trying to claim it for themselves, came up with an unlikely story involving a 'good Christian' and a pope. Almost certainly, it was first developed in England.

Withies

tough, flexible branches of an osier or other willows suitable for tying, binding or basketry.

Worcester Permain

of the many varieties of apple grown in the county, the Worcester Pearmain remains the most popular. An early season cultivar, first developed in Worcester by a Mr Hale of Swanpool in 1874, it is a smallish, bright red apple with a sweet strawberry flavour, which is able to flourish in most conditions.

Wort

the unfermented liquid extracted from the 'mashing' (crushing) process during the brewing of beer. It contains the sugars ('malts') that will then be fermented by the brewing yeast to produce alcohol.

SELECT BIBLIOGRAPHY

Archives:

Warwick County Record Office:

CR1153/2 Bidford Junior School Log Book, 1913-1928
CR0830 Bidford Infant School Log Book, 1891-1918
CR2376 /1 Bidford Infant School Log Book, 1918-1932
CR2376/5 Bidford Infant School Admissions Registers, 1913-1953
CR2191/3 Day Book of a Bidford Market Gardener

Broom Archives Group:

Irene Williams, Broom Scrapbook, Vol 5 (ed)

Newspapers:

Alcester Chronicle
Birmingham Daily Post
Evesham Journal
Evesham Standard
Leamington Spa Courier
Tamworth Herald
Tewkesbury Register and Agricultural Gazette
Warwick and Warwickshire Advertiser

Reference works:

Kelly's Directories, Warwickshire, 1896-1940
England and Wales National Census, 1871-1911
England and Wales National Register, 1939
J Wright and E Wright, The English Dialect Dictionary, 6 Vols, 1898-1905
J C Loudon, An Encyclopaedia of Agriculture, 1835

Books:

F Archer	*The Distant Scene*, 1967
	Under the Parish Lantern, 1969
	Grain and Chaff under the Hill, 1991
	A Country Twelvemonth, 1992
	Hay Days, 2001
J Bate	*John Clare: a Biography*, 2003
Bidford and District History Society	*Yesterday's Children*, 2013
C A Binyon	*The LBG Story*, 1958
R Churchley	*Having a Drink Round Bidford*, 2012
A Howkins	*Reshaping Rural History: A Social History, 1850-1925*, 1991
R Marshall	*We Will Remember Them*, 2014
R Marshall	*Have You Forgotten Yet?* 2018
H Newby	*Country Life: A Social History of Rural England*, 1987
M Pugh	*Shall We Dance? A Social History of Britain Between the Wars*, 2009
F Thompson	*Lark Rise to Candleford*, 1979 edition

Articles:

R Churchley	'Hard Times in Bidford-on-Avon', *Local Past*, Winter 1981/2, Alcester Historical Society.
H R Haggard	*Rural England*, extract in (www.badseysocietyuk/market-gardening-and-farming/rider-haggards-agricultural-survey-the-vale-of-evesham).
R Munday	'How Farming Suffered Post-World War I from the Government's Great Betrayal', in *Farmer's Weekly*, November 1918 (www.fwi-co.uk/news/how-farming-suffered-post-WWI-from-governments-betrayal).

INDEX FOR AVON ALMANAC

Please note that all items marked in ***italics*** *within the book are separately detailed in alphabetical order within the* ***Glossary****.*

The Index is divided into eight main sub-sections.
Within **Places** three additional sub-sections are included for **Bidford**: Public Houses and Hotels, Schools, and Shops and Businesses.

Notes

Notes

Notes

Planting Field Cabbages On A Smallholding
(The Book of Market Gardening, R. Lewis Castle 1906 - Wikimedia Commons)